OUR GARDENS

BY

S. REYNOLDS HOLE

AUTHOR OF

" A BOOK ABOUT ROSES," " MEMORIES OF DEAN HOLE," ETC

LONDON

J. M. DENT & CO., ALDINE HOUSE

29 & 30 BEDFORD STREET, W.C.

1907

Ridentem dicere verum
Quid vetat?

THE DEAN'S GARDEN, ROCHESTER.

CONTENTS

LIST OF ILLUSTRATIONS

The Author offers his sincere thanks to Lady FALMOUTH, *for the plan of Rose-Garden at Mereworth Castle, and to the* Hon. ALICE DOUGLAS-PENNANT, Sir W. THISELTON DYER, *Director of the Royal Gardens at Kew,* Mr. WILLIAM ROBINSON, Mr. F. H. EVANS, *for Photographs; and much regrets that want of space has prevented the introduction of those kindly sent by the Dean of Canterbury and by the Rector of Stonyhurst College. He also desires to thank* Mr. GEORGE ELGOOD *for permission to reproduce two of his Paintings.*

OUR GARDENS

CHAPTER I

The Enjoyments of a Garden

" Nature never did betray
The heart that loved her : 'tis her privilege
Through all the scenes of this our life to lead
From joy to joy."
　　　　　　　　　　—WORDSWORTH.

I ASKED a schoolboy, in the sweet summer-tide, "what he thought a garden was for?" and he said, *Strawberries*. His younger sister suggested *Croquet*, and the elder *Garden-parties*. The brother from Oxford made a prompt declaration in favour of *Lawn Tennis and Cigarettes*,

but he was rebuked by a solemn senior, who
wore spectacles, and more back hair than is
usual with males, and was told that "a garden
was designed for botanical research, and for
the classification of plants." He was about
to demonstrate the differences between the
Acoty- and the *Monocoty-ledonous* divisions, when
the collegian remembered an engagement elsewhere.

I repeated my question to a middle-aged
nymph, who wore a feathered hat of noble proportions over a loose green tunic with a silver
belt, and she replied, with a rapturous disdain of
the ignorance which presumed to ask—"What is
a garden for? For the soul, sir, for the soul
of the poet! For visions of the invisible, for
grasping the intangible, for hearing the inaudible,
for exaltations" (she raised her hands, and stood
tiptoe, like jocund day upon the misty mountain top, as though she would soar into space)
"above the miserable dulness of common life
into the splendid regions of imagination and
romance." I ventured to suggest that she would
have to do a large amount of soaring before
she met with anything more beautiful than the

flowers, or sweeter than the nightingale's note; but the flighty one still wished to fly.

A capacious gentleman informed me that nothing in horticulture touched him so sensibly as green peas and new potatoes, and he spoke with so much cheerful candour that I could not be angry; but my indignation was roused by a morose millionaire, when he declared that of all his expenses he grudged most the outlay on his confounded garden.

Dejected, I sought solace from certain ladies and gentlemen, who had expressed in my hearing their devoted love of flowers. They were but miserable comforters. Their devotion was superficial, their homage conventional: there was no heart in their worship. I met with many who held flowers in high estimation, not for their own sake, not for the loveliness and perfect beauty of their colour, their fragrance, and their form, not because even Solomon in all his glory was not arrayed like one of these, but because they were the most effective decorations of their window-sills, apartments, and tables, and the most becoming embellishments for their own personal display. I found gentlemen who restricted their enthusiasm to one class of plants, ignoring all the rest; and even in this their valuation was regulated by the rarity and the cost of the flower. "I can assure you, my dear sir," they said, "that there is only one other specimen in the country, and that the happy possessor is my friend, Lord Lombard." And I shall never forget the disastrous results which followed, when I informed one of these would-be monopolists, that I knew a third party, who had duplicates. He favoured me with a scowl of mingled disgust and doubt, sulked during the remainder of our interview, and became my bitter enemy for life.

> " Such men as he are never at heart's ease,
>   While they behold a greater than themselves."

Others were quite as exclusive, but with a difference of intention. They not only desired to possess, but that the public should know that they possessed, something out of the common; and from their love of renown, or their " *sacra auri fames*," they competed for the prizes which were awarded to their favourite flower. It seemed to me that they derived much more gratification from the cups and stakes than from the horses, who had won the race.

The unkindest cut of all, so common that it makes one callous, comes from those visitors who "would be so delighted to see our garden!" and they come and see, and forget to be delighted. They admire the old city walls which surround it, they like to hear the cawing of the rooks, they are pleased with the sun-dial and the garden-chairs, but as for horticulture they might as well be in Piccadilly! They would be more attracted by the fruit in Solomon's shop than by all the flowers in the border. I heard a lady speaking to her companion of "the most perfect gem she had ever seen," and when, supposing that reference was made to some exquisite novelty in plants, I inquired the name and habitation, I was informed that the subject under discussion was "Isabel's new baby!" "Ladies," I remarked, with a courteous but scathing satire, "I have been a baby myself, and am now a proprietor, but I am constrained to inform you that this is a private, and not a nursery, garden."

Thus disappointed, deceived, disheartened, I began to fear that my intense love of a garden might be a mere hallucination, an idiosyncrasy, a want of manliness, a softening of the brain. Nevertheless I persevered in my inquiries, until I found that which I sought—the sympathy of an enthusiasm as hearty as my own, a brotherhood and a sisterhood, who, amid all the ignorance and pretence of which I have given examples, were devoted to the culture of flowers, and enjoyed from this occupation a large portion of the happiness, which is the purest and the surest we can know on earth, the happiness of Home.

I received this sympathy from all sorts and conditions of men, and wherever I found it, the right hand of fellowship was held out to welcome. Sometimes that hand was huge, and hard, and discoloured: sometimes it was small and white. In some cases its operations were limited to a few window-plants, to a couple of grimy frames in a back yard, to a small cottage or allotment garden; and in others they had a wider range, in the suburbs, the villa of the tradesman, the mansion of the merchant, by the farmhouse, the parsonage, the hall, the castle, and the palace. Here there was a "greenhouse" not bigger than a four-post bed, and there a conservatory with a glittering dome, and spacious transepts, and a fountain, which never condescended to play except in the presence of distinguished "company." The disparity between the two extremes is striking, the contrast of the crystal corridors at the castle with the glazed box in the slums, but I am of opinion that quite as much affection, solicitude, and admiration were bestowed upon the auriculas as were given to the orchid or the palm. The great wax-doll, with its golden curls, which opens and shuts its deep blue eyes, and gives imitations of "Ma-ma," about as successful as the *Vox Humana* stop in an organ, is not more beloved by the sweet little lady (a size larger than itself) who holds it, than the hairless, armless, noseless wooden effigy, attired in the remnant of an old penwiper, which has been secured by a nail to its spine, is dear to little Sal in the alley.

In all these attachments there was the same enthusiasm, the same tender patience which watched the drooping plant, which "would sit up all night with a sick cactus," and the same proud exultation of the owner, when the flowers were in bloom, as though he were the sole patentee, and all their symmetry and perfume his own idea.

There are, of course, degrees of enjoyment, just as there are degrees of enthusiasm, of brains, and of income; but it may be accepted as a rule that they appreciate most heartily the rest and beauty of a garden, who have not only hard work to do outside of it, but use their hands to promote, as well as their eyes to admire, its charms. Sir Isaac Newton, who, so writes his biographer, Sir D. Brewster, could not endure the sight of a weed, would have rejoiced to admire their cleanly beds. All is in order without sign of artifice. Exuberance has been pruned or trained; fractures amputated or bound; moribund plants prematurely cremated.

Not long ago I paid a visit to my friend, Frank Goodhart (*nom de plume*, but an accurate description of the man), who has a small but charming garden some twenty miles out of London, wherein, before he leaves home for his daily work in a Government office, and when he returns from town, he spends his leisure time. Here I found him late on a summer's eve, and a healthier, happier, hotter, or dirtier person, I do not remember to have met in the society to which he belongs. As for his apparel, I was constrained to state that I could not have believed that a man of his ancient lineage and liberal education would have robbed a scarecrow, were I not positively convinced in my own mind that I had seen his jacket on duty. He only replied with a peremptory direction that I was to "catch hold" of two huge watering-cans, fill them from a tank some fifty yards away, and bring them back *toute suite*. For an hour I wobbled up and down his walks between these ponderous utensils, until the dressing-bell rang, and my friend, having made himself a C.B., resumed his ordinary aspect as an English gentleman.

During dinner we made a few preliminary remarks upon minor matters, such as wars, politics, education, and the labour question,

> " We spoke of other things ; we coursed about
> The subject most at heart, more near and near
> Like doves about a dovecote, whirling round
> The central wish, until we settled there."

I need hardly say that *the* subject was the garden and the dovecote under the verandah.

"Now is not this," said my host, when we had lighted our pipes, "simply delicious? I don't mean the tobacco, though it is the best which I brought from Virginia, but the sensation and the scene—above us 'the floor of heaven, thick inlaid with patens of bright gold,' and around us constellations even more beautiful to our eyes—

'Stars, which on earth's firmament do shine.'

"What a transmigration from dusky lane and wrangling mart, from sums and statistics, red tape, blank walls, dirty floors, and crowded streets, to this sweet restful home! When I left the office this afternoon, Green 'thought that he would have time for a couple of rubbers at the Club' (Green's whist is much admired at the Club by his opponents) 'before he dined with old Pomery at the Cecil.' Brown was engaged to a series of 'At Homes,' ingenious efforts to put twenty horses into a four-stall stable, and would spend much of his night on the stairs; Black had promised to preside at a meeting for the abolition of Taxes and Tithes; and White, who is a Christian Socialist, was going to the

Dustmen's Ball. All these gentlemen were to inhale an atmosphere more or less tainted by gas and other contaminations, and to go 'bedward ruminating,' when the night was far spent, to slumbers feverish and perturbed. And I am permitted (Heaven alone knows why) to come away from those tedious and costly disappointments, to breathe an unpolluted air, to maintain my health in its integrity by opening the pores of my skin" (I had never seen pores more porous), "to gladden my eyes with the fairest, and my nose with the sweetest, of all sights and scents; above all, I trust, to refine my taste, improve my mind, quicken my gratitude, and confirm my faith."

He paused, and as the sun retired behind a cloud of smoke, the moon took up the wondrous tale. *Respondere paratus* I continued the song of praise, and maintained the superiority of horticulture over all our other recreations. I reminded him that while no two men appreciated more keenly the joyful excitements, which were associated with horses and hounds, guns and rods, bats and balls, we knew that these delights were uncertain, transitory, and with long intervals between; that even for those, who had the inclination, the money, and the leisure to obtain them without restraint, there were manifold disappointments and vexations of spirit, blank days, hard frosts, vulpecides, wire fences, rotten banks, epidemics among grouse, mists on the mountains, impossible woodcocks, balls which broke in and salmon which broke off, with a power which no science could withstand; and that to all, be their failures many or few, there comes the inevitable hour when the bravest heart loses some of its courage, and the sight which was longest, and the arm which was strongest, predominate no more; but the garden never fails to produce, and the true gardener never fails to appreciate, its treasures. He is always hungry, because increase of appetite doth grow with that it feeds on, and the food is plentiful and cheap. He may be said to be the largest of landed proprietors, seeing that whenever he enters a garden, he enjoys its pleasures with the owner, and, as a rule, has the larger share.

If we pass from the ornamental to the useful, does not horticulture supply us not only with that which is pleasant to the sight but with that which is good for food, with our most wholesome and indispensable diet, our vegetables and fruit? How sadly would the excellent repast, which we have just now enjoyed, have deteriorated without these adjuncts! No tomatoes for the soup, no cucumber for the salmon, no new potatoes, no crisp salad, no mint sauce for the lamb, no peas for the duck, no apples for the tart, no radish for the cheese, no strawberries for the dessert. It has been said that all this produce may be more conveniently and economically supplied by the greengrocer, whom Theodore Hook described as "the Cock Pomona of the neighbourhood"; but when his goods have been freely manipulated by subalterns, who dislike ablution, and have travelled a few miles over dusty roads, they are no more to be compared with those from your own garden than a turnip with "a Queen" pineapple.

We discoursed on other advantages which accrue from horticulture. Troops of friends, in cottages and castles, with pretty souvenirs of friendship. The opportunity for those who have small houses and small incomes to enter-

tain their neighbours *al fresco*, for social intercourse, for a lecture or entertainment to promote
some charitable design. For the distribution of
fruit and flowers in the summer, of seeds and
plants in the autumn, of soup in the winter,
among the poor. The lessons of patience and
hope which we learn, a very present help in
trouble, in the sorrowful trials of life, in our
separations from those who were nearest and
dearest—the lessons which are taught us by the
fall of the leaf, the fading of the flower, by all
the decay and disappearance which so closely
resemble death; and then, after the sleep and
the snow-white shroud, the glorious revival of
the Spring !

> " The world of matter in its various forms
> All dies into new life, life out of death :
> Shall man alone, for whom all else revives,
> Imperial man, no resurrection know ! "

During our discourse we were delighted by an
announcement,

> " It is the hour when from the boughs
> The nightingale's high note is heard,"

followed by a performance of exquisite music,
and reminding us that the garden had charms

for the ear as well as for the eye and the nose, and that, after this delicious harmony had ceased, there would on the morrow be morning and afternoon concerts by the most distinguished soloists, "the mellow ousel fluting in the elm," and a magnificent chorus of song.

The utterance of the rook has a soothing if not a dulcet tone; and even the incessant chatter of the jackdaws, snappish, insolent, and specially obnoxious to those who are conversant with their contentious, aggressive, and thievish habits, is nevertheless associated with wise warnings for us, who dwell with them in the precincts of our cathedrals, not to deceive ourselves with vain imaginations that much speaking, or a combative spirit, or a constant familiarity with sacred things, will conduce to righteousness without that most excellent gift of charity—

> "A man may cry 'Church, Church' at every word,
> With no more piety than other people;
> A daw's not reckoned a religious bird,
> Because it keeps a cawing from the steeple."[1]

---

[1] Unless the little child was right, of whom White tells us in his History of Selborne, that when she heard the cawing of the rooks, she thought that "they were saying their prayers," having as her authority, though she knew it not, the inspired words, "He feedeth the ravens that call upon Him."

B

It must be confessed that some of the most
accomplished minnesingers have pugnacious and
predatory instincts, and are wont to wet their
whistles on the cherries, as a famous prima
donna upon London stout, before they begin
to warble; but our time will be better occupied
in frustrating these free-traders by the protection
of our fruit with nets rather than by preaching,
like St. Francis, to the birds.   Even where they
are free to pillage, they do more good than harm
by their diet of worms and their destruction of
all manner of flies.   They are cheerful companions; and if we have been disappointed to
find that the attendant robin, who approached
us so closely as we used the spade or the hoe,
was not attracted, as we once supposed, by our
personal charms; if we have been pained to
notice, when distributing food to our feathered
friends in the season of frost and famine, a lively
inclination among the recipients to peck out each
other's eyes, we may not forget that *animal
implume*, the lord of all creation, is occasionally
misled by selfish inclinations, and that civilised
and even Christian people have not been re-
strained by refinement or religion from annexing

the property and mutilating the persons of their fellow-men.

Remembering only the benefits and delights which the birds bestow, we shall find, as Addison found, a full compensation for their petty larcenies, as we listen to their song. "My garden," he writes, "invites into it all the birds of the country by offering them the conveniency of springs and shades, solitude and shelter, and I do not suffer any one to destroy their nests in spring, or drive them from their usual haunts in fruit-time. I value my garden more for being full of blackbirds than cherries, and very frankly give them fruit for their songs. By this means I have always the music of the season in its perfection, and am highly delighted to see the jay or the thrush hopping about my walks, and shooting before my eyes across the little alleys and glades." In the same spirit, that genial philosopher, Sir Richard Owen, replied to a friend of mine, who asked, when walking in his garden, why some of the cherries were not protected by nets, "They are the salaries of my orchestra, the wages of my choir."

We concluded our eulogium of horticulture

by assuring each other, though it was a work
of supererogation, that the "simple joys which
Nature yields" were not only the sweetest but
the most abiding of all, and that the true love
of a garden, which no money could buy, no
authority confer,

> " Quid pure tranquillet honos, an dulce lucellum.
>   An secretum iter, et fallentis semita vitæ ? "

would never cease to bless.

Then, with a sublime compassion for all those
belated persons who had not our enthusiasm, we
went to bed, and the nightingale sang us to
sleep.

CHAPTER II

Ignorance

*" I am the Master of a College,
And what I don't know is not knowledge."*
—Oxford Rhymes.

THE enjoyments of a garden being so manifold and continuous, bringing brightness to the home, health to the body, and happiness to the mind, it is for us, who have proved them, whose daily lives are made more cheerful by their influence, out of our gratitude and our goodwill, to invite and to instruct others, that they may share our joy.   There is great need of such persuasion.   These enjoyments, available in some degree to all, are accepted by few.   The desire, the capacity to enjoy, is an instinct; the love of flowers is innate, a remembrance of Eden ; but

these appreciations are too often expelled by
stronger excitements, and "the tender grace of a
day that is dead" comes back no more; in its
place evasion and excuse. "I have no time for
my garden," says the man who has ample leisure
for other relaxations. "Such pursuits are incompatible with important business and hard work;"
but our Colonial Secretary of State wears an
orchid, and the Nottingham mechanic a rose, in
his coat. "I am fond of flowers, but I know
nothing about them:" you are not fond, or
you would know. "I don't like the trouble:"
the labour we delight in physics pain. "I can't
stand the expense:" with twenty penny packets
of seed you may cover a rood of ground. Some
seem to regard horticulture as effeminate, beneath
the dignity of manhood, inconsistent with its
sporting instincts; but I have known horsemen
foremost with the Quorn and the Pytchley,
and soldiers and sailors brave in battle, who were
devoted gardeners. We hear no such weak
apologies, where there is a true affection. Going
in and out of London, and surveying the back
premises of crowded streets, we see here and
there, with long and dismal intervals of rubbish

and disorder, what zeal and cleanliness and constant care can do—the grass-plot about the size
of a sheet, the old stunted tree, which grew once
in the open field, the climbers on the walls, the
arbour, the flowers, few and far between, and the
canary singing from his cage, as though earth
had no fairer scene.

As a rule indifference, not so condensed, and
therefore not so obtrusive, prevails elsewhere,
and that true admiration of the beautiful, which
must have something to admire, is but seldom
seen, although the surroundings suggest, and the
means abound. There is no country in which
so large a proportionate space is occupied by
gardens, and there is no country in which,
owing to the fertility and variety of its soil, the
(comparatively) mild alternations of climate, the
industrious skill of the gardener *al fresco* and
under glass, the ubiquitous zeal of the traveller
in search of plants for importation,—so much
cultural success might be achieved.

In his charming treatise on the garden, Sir
William Temple writes: "I must needs add
one thing more in favour of our climate, which
I heard the king say, and I thought new and

right, and truly like a king of England, that loved and esteemed his own country. It was in reply to some of the company, that were reviling our climate, and extolling those of Italy, Spain, and France. He said, he thought that was the best climate, where he could be abroad in the air with pleasure, or at least without trouble and inconvenience, the most days of the year, and the most hours of the day; and that he thought he could be in England, more than in any country he knew of in Europe. 'And I believe it is true,' he said, 'not only of the hot and cold, but even among our neighbours in France and the Low Countries themselves, where the heats and the colds, and changes of seasons, are less treatable than they are with us.'

"There are, besides the temper of our climate, two things peculiar to us, which contribute much to the beauty and elegance of our gardens, which are the gravel of our walks, and the fineness, and almost perpetual greenness of our turf. The first is not known anywhere else, which leaves all their dry walks in other countries very unpleasant and uneasy; the other cannot be found in France or in Holland as we have it, the soil

not admitting that fineness of blade in Holland,
nor the sun that greenness in France."

Few in proportion avail themselves of these
advantages of soil and climate. There are delectable exceptions, but as a rule we find apathy,
neglect, or a meagre and monotonous repetition
in our horticulture. An immense majority of
those who possess large gardens are the passive
slaves of their gardeners, incapable of giving
directions, afraid to suggest them, lest they
should expose their ignorance. The peer, the
baronet, the squire, is his own Master of the
Horse, and can give orders to his stud-groom
with all the confidence of knowledge and with
all the dignity of power; he knows the pedigree
of his thoroughbreds, the specialities of every
steed which he rides or drives. In his presence
the head gamekeeper, elsewhere a man of arro-
gant demeanour, enriched by the "tips" and
flattered by the familiarity of the gunners, makes
the meek obeisance of true respect to his em-
ployer, who can marshal a troop of beaters, or
break a retriever, or bring down a rocketer, as
well as he can; but he stands before his gardener
speechless—cannot remember whether he was

instructed by his wife to insist on more flowers for the room or more room for the flowers, and dare not fulfil his promise to the farm-bailiff to reduce the extravagant amount of manure which is demanded for the garden.

The farmer, like the farm-bailiff, attests his determination to bestow upon his fields exclusively the precious contributions of his yard, his stable, and his sty, and is rarely induced, by a wife who can preserve fruit or a daughter who can appreciate flowers, to make a small donation, grudgingly and as of necessity, from his fertilising stores. His orchard, outside the counties of Hereford, Worcester, and Kent, is a desolation.

The clergy, as a class, may claim precedence in horticulture, like their ecclesiastical brethren of old, not because they can boast of many gardeners famous for their knowledge and culture of plants, such as Canon Ellacombe and the Rev. C. Wolley-Dod, but because, as with the mediæval monks, their ignorance is less profound, and their apathy less supine, than in any other community. In proportion to their numbers, there are more clergymen than laymen who know the difference between a Mallow and a

Salpiglossis, a Prunus Pisardi and a Copper
Beech.

What is the explanation? So much profession,
so little practical zeal; so much verbiage, so
little work; so many gardens, so few gardeners;
so many eyes colour-blind, so many ears which
never listen to the song of the birds, the hum
of the bees, the sough of the wind, or the
murmur of the stream; so many noses which
never smell the violet or the rose; so many
hands which have never sown a seed, never
planted a root, never plucked a flower. Why
in so many grounds are the trees and shrubs
permitted to crowd, disfigure, and destroy each
other? Why are they left unpruned, untrained,
cankered, decayed, exhausted, barren, and reverting to type? Why in countless instances is
there no hoe, no water in the time of drought,
no protection for the tender in the bitter frost,
no manure for the exhausted soil, so that we
mourn for their privations, as Dick Swiveller
mourned for "the Marchioness," brought up in
ignorance of the taste of beer.

I know the answer which would be given by
a large number of respondents, if they spoke the

truth : " We should regard it as a favour if you
would cease to bore us with your dickey-birds
and daffidowndillies. We believe in your peaches,
we appreciate your salads, your early strawberries
and peas; we do not object to your flowers in
moderation; but we really cannot interest ourselves in your guano and garden rollers. We
do not care to associate with "the worms that
creep in and the worms that creep out," except
in the form of baits; and while we do not for a
moment dispute your perfect freedom to spend
your leisure hours among the caterpillars, the
red spiders, and the mealy bugs, we must claim
for ourselves the same liberty to seek amuse-
ments which are more congenial to our tastes,
and which do not require at frequent intervals
the fumigator or the squirt."

I remember my Latin lessons, and in unpleasant circumstances I preserve an equal mind.
I reply, with that gentle tenderness which one
always feels for the blind, that, so far from being
surprised or irritated, I am touched by a sincere
sympathy and by a thankful joy. I have passed
through the same experience, the same thoughts
have occupied my mind, the same words have

expressed them. I recall a period when, in the enthusiastic language of youth, all the recreations which I liked were "ripping," and all those which I disliked were "rot." The man who ventured to admire such ordinary rubbish as scenery, sunsets, and flowers, was denounced as a "duffer," and his conversation was "bosh." The only florist whom we recognised was the purveyor of bouquets at a guinea apiece for presentation to the belles of the ball, or of dainty "button-holes" at two-and-six for our own personal adornment. Yes, my dear friends, I can assure you that I have slept the same placid, I might almost say porcine, slumbers, which possess you now; and in the same condition of profound ignorance have dreamed, as you are dreaming, that I had all knowledge   Hence my compassion for your sad estate, and my gratitude for the bright awaking which delivered me from darkness, and which, without diminishing any other enjoyments, conferred upon me the sweetest and the surest of them all. Let me earnestly invite you to "shake off dull sloth, and early rise" to see and to share this happiness, to apprehend the beauty which surrounds you, the grandeur, the order, the exquisite perfection, from the giant Sequoia to the tiny lichen, from the cedar which is in Lebanon even to the hyssop which springeth out of the wall. You have only to search until you have found some single flower which attracts and absorbs your admiration, and that thing of beauty shall be your joy for ever. You will have entered a land which is the glory of all land, Araby the blest, which has no bounda̅ es. Once taste the delights of a garden, and they will never fail to please. The cloud, no bigger than a man's hand, shall be followed by a gracious and abundant rain. My own conversion came from a flower, which I shall never forget, more than half a century ago; and I know several instances in which the perusal of a book, the sight of a neighbour's garden, a visit to a floral exhibition, have transformed indifference into zeal.

CHAPTER III

The Pioneers

" Men come to build stately sooner than to garden finely."—LORD BACON.

THIS indifference, being coeval with ignorance, is of ancient date in England. The Latin historian, Strabo, informs us that the Britons in the first century knew nothing about horticulture, although a few were wont to designate certain portions of their lands as gardens; but they doubtless derived at this period considerable information from their Roman visitors. The poet (oh rare Ben Jonson!) tells us of a time—

> " In Rome's poor age,
> When both her kings and consuls held the plough,
> And gardened well,"

and we know that, when Rome was rich, enormous sums were lavished on the gardens, which surrounded the marble palace of the villa, and that many of her most famous sons—rulers, warriors, philosophers, and poets—rejoiced in their cultivation.   But, though they began to build stately, they never began to garden finely, except in the production of " fine herbs."   They devoted themselves almost exclusively to the kitchen department, and were literally market gardeners, not only growing vegetables tor their own consumption, but sending them to Rome for sale.   They were glad, as some of our magnates now, to defray part of the labourer's wages from the results of his toil.   Their success was in proportion to their zeal, and was esteemed to be of such honourable merit and distinction, that Cicero, Fabius, Lentulus, and Piso derived their appellations from their skilful treatment of the vetch, the bean, the lentil, and the pea.   The Emperor Diocletian is said to have contemplated his cabbages with even more enjoyment than the agonies of the Christians, whom he slowly tortured to death.   Cato was supreme in asparagus, and Columella in the culture of the vine.   The

Romans would therefore make large and delectable additions to the vegetable diet of the Briton, which consisted mainly of acorns, and the greatest of their generals, Julius *Agricola*, would be indeed the farmer's friend. Imagine the voracious relish with which these hungry savages would consume their new and palatable food, the first intensity of their delight, which has come down to us through the ages, in the combination of bacon and beans!

The victors enlightened the untutored minds of the vanquished, as when the shutters are opened in a dark room. They taught them how to fight, and convinced them of the superiority of armour to blue paint in the noble art of self-defence. They showed them how to make those straight and level roads, of which we have still remains, through the length and breadth of the land. They instructed them not only in the growth and use of corn and vegetables, but of vines, figs, mulberries, apricots, cherries, and other fruits hitherto unknown to them. They made laws for the lawless, and even went so far as to intimate that there were such things as manners. They bade them " dig and bore the solid earth, and from the strata there extract" the tin, as in Cornwall, the lead in Somerset, the iron in Northumberland and in the Forest of Dean; but there was one subject on which they had nothing to say, being themselves profoundly ignorant, and *ex nihilo nihil fit.* They could not teach floriculture, simply because they were not florists. The spacious grounds, as extensive in many cases as our English parks, such as those of Tarquin the Superb, Lucullus, Cicero, Sallust, Nero, Pliny, and of Adrian at beautiful Tivoli, which all who go to Rome should see, were splendid specimens of architectural talent and of hydraulic skill, but they never deserved, according to our idea and definition, the name of gardens. They were chiefly composed of terraces, balustrades, steps, porticos, cupolas, colonnades, alcoves, summer-houses, statues, pyramids, vases, obelisks, lakes —some of them large enough for the representation in miniature of naval engagements (note how history repeats itself at Olympia and Earl's Court)—cascades, and fountains. Sometimes there was a gymnasium; here and there a hippodrome or a theatre. Baths in abundance, hot and cold. There were groves, it is true; there were long lines of trees, principally planes; there were evergreen shrubs; but the latter were clipped into fantastic forms, into hideous resemblances of birds, and beasts, and creeping things of the earth. Flowers were only grown in small beds, edged with box, still continued in "the Dutch Garden," or in masses, as in our nurseries, for decoration, *neu desint epulis rosæ*, &c. They had this apology, that in numerous instances all the land around was covered with a carpet of lovely flowers, and that the beauty of nature was beyond the imitation of art. The representation of mountains, forests, and lakes by hillocks, clumps, and pools, is about as successful as children's castles on the sands.

Anarchy and ugliness returned to our island, when in the fifth century the Romans were compelled to leave it, the invaders to resist invasion, and took possession of the empty house, which had been swept and garnished. Here and at home Rome lost her empire.

> " The desolator desolate, the victor overthrown,
>   The arbiter of others' fate a suppliant for her own."

The barbarian won the battle all along the line.

Simultaneously, the Goth and the Vandal, the Pict, the Scot, and the Saxon, held the land, and swept the sea.

Our lively ancestors the pirates under Hengist landed in Kent, conquered it, crowned the three sons of their leader as kings, and proceeded to annex the rest of the country, and to exterminate the Britons. This process evoked considerable opposition from persons entertaining similar views with regard to appropriation, and there ensued a continuance of offensive and defensive warfare, which suppressed all hope of civilisation, and absorbed the ambition and the energy of mankind in dauntless efforts to perforate, slash, and crush each other with arrow, halberd, and ram. Mars and Bellona led the Dance of Death, Venus dwelt in the woods with the wild roses, or among the heather on the hills. Pomona eked out a precarious existence on blackberries, crabs, and nuts. Minerva was not to be found.

Passing seriously from gay to grave — the motive power of the only true civilisation, Christianity, was lost. The foundations had been laid, but the builders were gone. Long time, as in the days of Nehemiah, they had worked, now wielding weapons of defence, and now the mason's tools, but they had been for a while overcome of evil. They had been constrained to flee, and the British Church, the most ancient branch of the Catholic Church in our land, was exiled, with its bishops, priests, and people, to remote boundaries, such as the mountains of Wales, whither their persecutors declined to follow.

Out of the darkness of this long and stormy night shone the bright and morning star. The watchmen on the tower at Argos saw in the distance far away, the first beacon-flame of victory. The famished sentry caught the first notes, "too far off for the tune," of an army marching to save. Æthelbert, the heathen king of Kent, married Bertha, the Christian princess of Paris, and the Church of St. Martin at Canterbury was restored and reopened for worship. Thus encouraged, Gregory the Great, who had designed, it is said, a mission to England long before he became Bishop of Rome, and who had declared that some boys, whom he saw in the slave-market, ruddy and of a fair countenance, with blue eyes and golden hair, would be no longer "Angles, but angels, if they became Christians," sent Augustine with a band of faithful colleagues to contend earnestly for the faith once delivered to the saints.

At Ebbsfleet, the place where Hengist had come ashore with his pirates, Augustine disembarked some 150 years after, not with the shout of battle, the fury of the oppressor, and the clash of arms, but with psalms and hymns and spiritual songs, with prayers of penitence, with promises of pardon, with the offer of eternal peace. There was neither sword nor spear—a simple cross and a message from the Crucified, "Come unto Me, all ye that travail and are heavy laden, and I will give you rest."

This spring overflowed into a stream, and this stream, with other tributaries, formed the river "broad and deep, and brimming over," which rolls onward to the sea. The primitive church in Britain and Ireland, for which some claimed St. Paul as founder, some St. Joseph of Arimathea, and which all believe to have existed in or soon after Apostolic times, the Church of Sts. Ninian, Patrick, and Alban, was ultimately combined with the Church represented by St. Augus-

tine; and that Church gradually became the
dominant power in legislation, many centuries
before there was a Parliament, in the administra-
tion of justice, in the acquisition of knowledge,
and in the study of art. Ecclesiastics were not
only the rulers and the lawyers, the arbiters and
almoners, the architects, musicians, and painters,
of the nation, but they were the farmers and
gardeners also. They dug and drained, they
planted and sowed, they " made the desert smile."
Had there been no monasteries, no peaceful
homes, to which devout and intellectual men
could go for prayerful meditation, for reading
and research, for obedience to the immutable law,
" in the sweat of thy face thou shalt eat bread," to
bear one another's burden, to teach the ignorant,
and to relieve the poor, why, then, as Lord
Macaulay writes, there would have been only two
kinds of men in the land, slaves and tyrants,
beasts of burden and beasts of prey.

These brothers, these monks, of whom the
drunkards make song, and of whom lewd fellows
of the baser sort who never denied themselves a
mouthful of meat or drink, only speak in scorn
and derision, felled the trees, dug up the under-

wood, drained, ploughed, and sowed the soil, reaped and thrashed, ground and baked. They reared their sheep and cattle, they milked and churned, they arose, like St. Peter, to kill and eat. But their meals were chiefly of fish, vegetables, and fruit, and their horticultural energies were devoted almost exclusively to the *Herbarium* and the *Pomarium*, the kitchen garden and the orchard.

Not only the vegetables were grown in the *Herbarium*, for the daily food of the brethren, but a variety of medicinal herbs for themselves and their neighbours. They were, in most districts, the only physicians, apothecaries, and surgeons. They prescribed, and dispensed their prescriptions at the monastery gate. They remembered their Divine commission, not only to tend, but to heal—to care for the bodies as well as for the souls of men. Although they knew that

> " Contra vim mortis,
> Non est medicamen in hortis,"

they had been taught that " the Lord had created medicines out of the earth," and he that is wise will not abhor them, and, though they had learned nothing of antiseptics and anesthetics, they had received many gifts of healing, had discovered many alleviations of pain, many restorative drinks, many soothing salves, for the aches and disorders which flesh is heir to.   There were in those days a number of quacks and mountebanks, to whom might be applied Pitt's revised quotation from Shakespeare, after a speech by Addington, M.D.,

> " I do remember an apothecary
>   Gulling of simples,"

but the monks had many reliable remedies, and some of them, such as " dandelion tea," *taraxacum*, for disease of the liver, are still in use.   I have seen collections of herbs for medicines offered for sale in the marketplace at Nottingham.

There were vegetables in abundance, beans, beet, cabbages, cucumbers, fennel, garlic, leek, kale, lettuce, mint, onions, parsley, peas, radishes, turnips, for these were necessaries of life, and the necessity which arises from hunger is the most prolific mother of invention.   I have known Englishmen, who were utterly incapable of conversation in the French language, and who would have preferred to hide themselves in secret

places rather than to have made experiments in
that direction, quite voluble in their instructions
to the waiter as to their selections from the *ménu*
and the *carte de vins*.

In the *Pomarium* they had a variety of excellent fruit, for immediate consumption, for pies
and puddings, cider, and preserves—apples, pears,
plums, cherries, mulberries, and nuts.

In the precincts at Rochester we have a plot
of ground which is still known as "The Vines,"
and in "the Vine-fields" at Hereford and elsewhere we are reminded of the monastic vine-
yards. It was possible by the selection of site
and soil, by surroundings of walls or hedges, by
manuring and hoeing, by training, pruning, and
thinning, to produce grapes, which, though never
large, were sweet and wholesome, and with some
little assistance, such as that which is given to
the cowslip, the elderberry, the cherry, and the
gooseberry, would make a pleasant and refreshing wine; but in a country so oft "deformed by
sullen rains," and liable to ten degrees of frost in
May, the *al fresco* vinery was vanity and vexation
of spirit, and was abandoned on the introduction
of glass-houses, and the importation of wines

from lands which were more familiar with the
sun. It pleases certain persons to represent the
inmates of a monastery as bloated with rich viands
and blotched with alcohol, as singing *da capo* this
perpetual song,

> " O quam bonum est !
> O quam jucundum est !
> Poculis fraternis gaudere ! "

but in all cases for many centuries, and in all
cases as a rule, the diet was too plain and sparse,
and the labour too hard, for obesity; and as to
the wine, it must have frequently resembled the
" *Chasse-Cousin* " with which the French are said
to banish the guests who are becoming tedious.
Something like it has been introduced into this
country as " a good sound dinner drink," or as
" a remarkably pure Moselle," at 10s. per dozen.

As to floriculture, these brethren, who believed
that

> " 'Tis good to work as well as to pray,"

had neither the time nor the taste for ornamental gardening. They grew a large quantity of
flowers, some in beds bordered with box, almost
exclusively for church decoration, for their altars
and shrines, for marriages, for the graves of the

departed. Sometimes the priests wore floral garlands, and it is on record that at the consecration of a bishop at St. Paul's Cathedral in 1405, the canons walked in procession crowned with roses.

It is still the custom, when the judges pay their annual visit to St. Paul's, for the canons to carry bouquets in their hands, but a similar embellishment of the head would bring all London to see. Nevertheless this ancient coronation might be suggestive and helpful to some gay young ritualist, yearning to irritate the Protestant mind, and a garland of sunflowers or a wreath of dahlias could hardly fail to succeed.

Roses, lilies, violets, narcissus, and iris were the favourite flowers of the garden, and then as now there was an abundance of indigenous beauty in the woods and fields.

So it came to pass that in the culture of the soil as in the culture of the soul, in the education of the mind and the treatment of the body, of *mens sana in corpore sano*, in the discoveries of science and in the accomplishments of art, the ecclesiastics had no rival. Outside the monasteries very few could read or write. The majority were occupied in killing one another, or in the pursuit of wild animals with hound and bow. They must have had splendid sport— no certificates, no preserves, no keepers, no wire fences, but wolves, wild boars, and stags, eagles and falcons, badgers and ferocious cats. There were no filthy infusions of drugs or of dyes to pollute the rivers and to poison the fish. But the monks, although they may occasionally have gratified the sporting instinct, girding their loins by tucking up their cassocks for the better supply of the larder and the stew, would only regard these exercises with the bow and the net as necessities or recreations, always remembering, as every rational being, most of all the Christian, is bound to remember, that we have duties to discharge as well as blessings to enjoy, and that every man, like Him in whose image he was made, has his trinity in unity, mind, body, spirit, or soul, and that each has its work to do, with all its awful responsibilities and its glories of joy and hope.

Surely it would have been wiser to have reformed instead of destroying the monasteries; to have pruned the branches instead of felling

the tree; to have maintained them as colleges
for the training of candidates for Holy Orders,
of schoolmasters and schoolmistresses, as asylums
for the aged, as convalescent homes, as reforma-
tories, instead of alienating for the enrichment
of royal favourites that which was intended for
the benefit of the nation, and of separating from
its sacred intentions that which had been given
to God.

CHAPTER IV

Progress

" Let us now praise famous men."
—ECCLESIASTICUS xliv.

CHRISTIANITY continued to extend its influence, its appreciations of justice, its obedience to authority, its longings for peace. Great kings such as Cnut and Edward the Confessor began to recognise their responsibilities, and to realise their power to do good.

There was a period of perturbation, when William, the irresistible—" no man could bend his bow "—came over with our illustrious ancestors—that is to say, with the ancestors of those who yearn for a first-class pedigree, are prepared to pay for it, and do not mind the hiatus of a few centuries, here and there; but gradually the people ceased to resent the inevitable, and there was a fusion of Britons, Angles, Saxons, and Danes with the brave Normans who had conquered them all. The hand of time joined them together, just as our little fingers in childhood united with triumphant joy the pieces of painted wood, with which we copied to completion the map or the picture before us.

Bede and Alfred created English literature. Our commerce prospered, and our ships with exports and imports were sailing over all the seas. The English language by degrees superseded the tongue of the invader.

Forests were felled, fens were drained, and as the people spread throughout the land, fields of green pasture and of golden corn gave beauty to the landscape and food for man and beast.

Horticulture followed agriculture.

"The penal curse
Was softened into mercies,"

and the flowers of the garden, like the wheat of the field, expelled the thistle and the thorn. Grim-visaged war had smoothed his wrinkled front, and Judah and Israel dwelt safely, every man under his vine and under his fig-tree, as in all the days of Solomon.

In the three centuries which followed the Norman Conquest, there were developments of ornamental culture. The first park known in England was made at Woodstock for King Henry I., and was surrounded by a wall. It is described as *habitatio ferarum*, and was mainly designed to be a preserve and covert for wild game. At a later period, in the reign of Henry II., the favourite garden of the royalty and nobility was the Bear-garden, in which these wretched animals were kept for periodical and public baiting, and from the twelfth century it seems to have been the chief holiday enjoyment of kings and commons to set their dogs on bulls and bears. "The Master of the King's Bears" was a royal appointment in the reign of Henry VIII., and Queen Elizabeth was so fascinated by their performances that, although she professed to be a devoted admirer of Shakespeare, in the year 1591 she caused an order to be issued by the Privy Council forbidding plays to be acted on

D

Thursdays, because that was the day which was generally preferred for the growling of the dogs, the bellowing of the bulls, and the roaring of the bears, as they worried and mangled each other. The lineaments of Sir Henry Irving, Mr. Beerbohm Tree, or Mr. Wilson Barrett, would be a study for the painter of portraits, were they to receive a similar injunction from her gracious Majesty Queen Victoria ; and yet it was not until 1835, only two years before she ascended the throne, that "the keeping of any house, pit, or other place, for baiting or fighting any bull, bear, dog, or other animal," was suppressed by Act of Parliament.

Despite their sanguinary habits, these cruel instincts, innate in all, exemplified by the schoolboy, who begins his entomological studies with a combat between the "soldier" and the "sailor" in a pillbox, who conveys the fly into the web of the spider, and shares the joy of his repast; in the sportsman, who exclaims at sunrise (so Charles Lamb writes), "Here's a fine day—let us kill something;" despite these truculent inclinations, inflamed by the hatreds and maddened by the carnage of continuous war; despite the

terrible destruction of life by the pestilence,
which had the awful designation of "the Black
Death," and which was so fatal among the farm
labourers, that there were not enough to cultivate
the land, much less the garden; despite the wars
between York and Lancaster, the Royalists and
the Puritans; there were many manifestations
in the Middle Ages, and especially after the
Restoration, of horticultural progress.

Gardens gradually increased around the palace,
and the castle, the hall, the grange, and the
suburban villa; but the process was slow, and
the productions were poor. At the beginning of
the sixteenth century the Earl of Northumberland
had an establishment of 160 persons, but only
one of these· a gardener, who attended "hourely
in the Garden for setting of herbis, and clipping
of knottis, and sweeping the said garden clene."

The formation and the arrangements of a
garden were a combination of the Roman and
monastic methods. The ornamental portion,
"the pleasure ground," was laid in straight lines
and squares, and was constructed almost entirely
by the architect, the sculptor, and the hydraulic
engineer. There were walks, terraces, steps,

balustrades, summer-houses, colonnades, and statues in abundance. There were lakes, ponds, and fountains. There were long lines of trees in monotonous repetition, but the shrubs, with the exception of evergreens, and the flowers in "knotts" and in parterres, were few.

The labyrinth, a maze of intricate and infinite paths between hedges of yew, box, and privet, was much in vogue, although the historical critic, who delights to assail our ancient impressions with his unpleasant facts, discredits Rosamond's Bower. Some of these had an elevation in the centre, on which a gardener was placed for the guidance of the bewildered inmates; to the great relief of frightened children who were beginning to meditate on the tragedy of "The Babes in the Wood," and of guests in the house, who heard the dressing-bell, and saw no exit in the direction of dinner; but to the surprise and discomfort of Edwin and Angelina, who would so much rather be lost than found.

The useful portion, the gardens for culinary and medicinal purposes, and the orchards for fruit, received much more careful and successful treatment than the flowers; and we find accordingly that the first books which were published with reference to gardens were the "Great Herbals," which treated almost exclusively of the properties and preparation of herbs, for physic and for food.

The most deplorable feature of these ancient gardens was the hewing and the hacking, the lopping and the clipping, of evergreen trees and shrubs. The mistakes of the Creator were to be rectified by the gardener's shears. The obtrusive and superfluous exuberance, the absurd irregularities, must be repressed and transformed. The complications, the twists, and the tangles must be removed. Ringlets must be combed straight; the head, cheek, lip, and chin of manhood must be shaven and shorn for "the convict cut."

> "Hence the sidelong walks
> Of shaven yew, the holly's prickly arms
> Trimmed into high arcades, the tonsile box,
> Wove in mosaic mode of many a curl
> Around the figured carpet of the lawn.
> Hence too deformities of harder cure,
> The terrace mound uplifted, the long line
> Of flat canal, deep delved ; and all that toil
> Misled by tasteless fashion could achieve
> To mar fair Nature's lineaments divine." [1]

---

[1] Mason's "English Garden."

These arrangements were generally admired as perfection, and it was a common boast that the English were inferior to none, in Italy, France, or Holland, in "the Topiary" or close-shaving department. Paradise itself was represented by an artist early in the seventeenth century as laid out in the height of the fashion, with the usual walks and squares, trees cut into patterns, and the last new things in water-works.

These water-works were not always suggestive of the felicities of Paradise to those who went to see. To drench the spectators by the adroit manipulation of a secret spring was regarded as a supreme triumph of engineering skill, a splendid effort of exquisite humour, and the brave but abortive efforts of the visitors, in their best bonnets and new hats, to look as though they liked it, evoked ecstasies of rapturous mirth from the spectators who had been previously irrigated, or had been privately warned. For the rest, there must have been great perturbations of spirit beneath the silk (watered) spencers of the ladies and the limp ruffles of the gentlemen, and a fierce combat between the impulses of a righteous wrath and that serene indifference towards all persons and incidents, including earthquakes, which distinguishes the members of genteel society.

And this reminds me of an incident. My son was in the public drawing-room of an hotel in Paris with a lady and her boy, a bright little fellow of some seven years. Suddenly the proprietor rushed into the apartment, white with rage, but evidently resolved to keep his indignation in subjection to his interest, and spoke from quivering lips: "A thousand pardons, my lady, but it is absolutely important that the little angel there shall not again derange the robinet, and flood the whole hotel." And he smiled a ghastly smile at the angel.

There were other frivolous adornments, fond things vainly invented. In Queen Elizabeth's garden in St. James's Park there was a grotto, made of all kinds of shells, representing Parnassus, with figures of Apollo and the Muses, and Pegasus at the top in full gallop. The hackney coachmen of the period must have contemplated this structure, complimented the nine ladies, and admired the horse, with much originality of thought and diction.

These whims, conchological and otherwise, were suggestive to coarser minds of a more culpable evtravagance, such as that which reached the climax of profane indecency, when in the year 1791 the proprietors of the gardens at Vauxhall erected a new gallery, in honour of their royal and frequent visitor, the Prince of Wales, in front of which was a transparent picture, representing his Royal Highness in armour, with Britannia leading his charger, Minerva holding his helmet, *Providence adjusting his spurs,* Fame crowning him with laurels and blowing the trumpet of his immortal honour and renown.

The night was long and dark, but "the stars shone o'er the cypress trees," and at last there came the dawn of day. Lord Bacon, "sagest Verulam," "the wisest, brightest, meanest of mankind," has been designated as "the Prophet" of the natural or English system of gardening; and no one can read his "Essay on Gardens," his declaration that a garden is the purest of human pleasures and the greatest refreshment to the spirit of man, without which buildings and palaces are but gross handiworks; his earnest admiration of colour, form, and fragrance; his declaration that "in the royal ordering of gardens there ought to be gardens for all the months in the year," followed by a long list of flowers, and shrubs, and trees, for cultivation from January to December, so that "you may have, if you will, the Golden Age again, and a Spring all the year round"; his appreciation of lawns and alleys, because "there is nothing more pleasant to the eye than green grass kept finely shorn"; his disdain of knots or figures with divers coloured earths, "because they be but toys," and of images cut out of juniper or other garden stuff, because "they be for children"; of pools, because "they make the garden unwholesome and full of flies and frogs";—no one can be reminded that he not only suggested these improvements but spared no cost to produce them, without admiring him as something more than a prophet, as a pioneer and guide in a new and beautiful land.

Nevertheless, my Lord Verulam was as one who comes suddenly from a darkened room into "the bickerings of the noontide blaze," and his sight was not strong enough to discern all the grace and glory of the scene before him. The prejudice of centuries, in which Art had followed its own imaginations instead of copying Nature, lingered in his brain and obscured his vision when he wrote: "The garden is best to be square, encompassed on all the four sides with a stately arched hedge. The arches to be upon pillars of carpenter's work, of some ten foot high and six foot broad; and the spaces between to be of the same dimensions with the breadth of the arch. Over the arches let there be an entire hedge of some four foot high, framed also upon carpenter's work. And over every arch, and upon the upper hedge over every arch, a little turret, with a belly, enough to receive a cage of birds. And over every span between the arches some little figure, with broad plates of round coloured glass for the sun to play upon!"

Milton was declared to be the poet laureate of the natural, or English garden, because he wrote:—

> " Flowers worthy of Paradise, which not mere art
> In beds and curious knots, but Nature born
> Poured forth profuse on hill, and dale, and plain."

And though this expression of a preference of Eden to all other gardens seems to be a superfluous repetition, it serves as a perpetual protest against those curious "knots," which were unknown until Paradise was Lost.

The prophet and the poet were succeeded by two famous men who, far below them as authors, were far before them as gardeners. At a time when it was gravely advised that "*flowers should be grown sparsely lest they should injure the roots of the trees*"; when beds were surrounded by painted rails; when it might be said—

> "The suffering eye inverted nature sees,
>   Trees cut to statues, statues thick as trees";

Addison wrote in the *Spectator*, June 25, 1712 "Our British gardeners, instead of humouring Nature, love to deviate from it as much as possible. Our trees rise in globes, cones, and pyramids. We see the marks of the scissors upon every plant and bush. I do not know whether I am singular in my opinion, but for my own part, I would rather look upon a tree in all its luxuriancy, with its diffusion of boughs and branches, than when it is thus cut and trimmed into a mathematical figure, and cannot imagine but that an orchard in flower looks infinitely more delightful than all the little labyrinths of the most finished *parterre*. But as our great modellers of gardens have their magazines of plants to dispose of, it is very natural for them to tear up all the beautiful plantations of fruit-trees, and contrive a plan that may turn to their own profit in taking off their evergreens and like movable plants with which their shops are plentifully stocked."

In the year following, September 29, 1713, Pope wrote in the *Guardian*: "We seem to make it our study to recede from Nature, not only in the various tonsure of greens into the most regular and formal shapes, but even in monstrous attempts beyond the reach of the art itself. We run into sculpture, and are yet better pleased to have our trees in the most awkward figures of men and animals than in the most regular of their own :—

> There slips of myrtle sail in seas of box,
> And there a green encampment meets the eye.

While persons of genius and those who are most capable of Art love Nature most, and are chiefly sensible that all Art consists in the imitation and study of Nature, people, on the contrary, of the common level of understanding are principally delighted with the little niceties and fantastical operations of Art, and constantly think that finest which is least Natural. A citizen is no sooner proprietor of a couple of yews, but he entertains thoughts of erecting them into giants, like those of Guildhall. I know an eminent cook, who beautified his country seat with a Coronation Dinner in Greens, where you see the champion flourishing on horseback at one end of the table, and the Queen in perpetual youth at the other." And then he commends, among other curiosities, "St. George in box; his arm scarce long enough, but will be in a condition to stick the dragon by next April." "A green dragon of the same, with a tail of ground ivy for the present. Edward the Black Prince in cypress. An old maid of honour in wormwood. And a quickset hog, shot up into a porcupine, having been forgot during a week of rainy weather."

Again he wrote, in his "Moral Essays" :—

"Lo! what huge heaps of littleness around!
The whole a laboured quarry above ground.
Two Cupids squirt before ; a lake behind
Improves the keenness of the northern wind.

His gardens next your admiration call:
On every side you look,—behold the wall !
No pleasing intricacies intervene,
No artful wildness to perplex the scene ;
Grove nods at grove, each alley has a brother,
And half the platform just reflects the other ".—

recalling the delicious story of my Lord Selkirk,
walking on a terrace in his garden in St. Mary's
Isle, which had a summer-house at either end.
In one of these he found a boy imprisoned for
stealing apples, and in the other a son of his
gardener, about the same age, looking out with
a doleful countenance. Meeting the father,
Lord Selkirk expressed his sorrow, supposing
that the boys were accomplices. " Nae, nae, my
lord," said the gardener, " my laddie's no thief,
but I just put him there for symmetry."

Pope had the courage of his opinions, and
practised that which he preached. He formed
a garden in consistent obedience to his own
golden rule—

" He wins all points who pleasingly confounds,
Surprises, varies, and conceals the bounds,"

following the graceful irregularities of Nature
rather than the precise mensurations of longitude

and latitude by line, rejecting vulgar frivolities, regarding Art as the humble handmaid of a mistress who required no cosmetics nor tight lacing—just a pin here and there, a brush and a comb, privately applied by an unseen hand—*ars est celare artem.*

Horace Walpole tells us that "Pope had so twisted and twirled, and rhymed and harmonised his few acres of ground at Twickenham, that he had formed two or three sweet little lawns opening and opening, one beyond another, and the whole surrounded by thick impenetrable woods. Sir William Stanhope, who bought Pope's house and garden, hacked and hewed these groves, wriggled a winding gravel walk through them, with an edging of shrubs, in what they call modern taste, and in fact desired the three lanes outside to walk in again, and now is forced to shut them out by a wall, for there was not a Muse could walk there but she was spied by any country fellow that went by with a pipe in his mouth."

Not satisfied with this demolition, done in the spirit of the victorious Goth who destroyed the great library because he could not read, the new

occupant added insult to injury; and when in
the summer of 1898 I went with my friend Mr.
William Robinson, the author of the "English
Flower Garden," on a pious pilgrimage to the
home of our Pope—not the Vatican—we were
perturbed by mixed feelings of mirth and indignation as we read on a boundary wall the lines,
signed "Clare," but affiliated to Stanhope,

> "This humble roof, the garden scanty line,
>   Ill spoke the genius of a bard divine;
>   But fancy now displays a fairer scope,
>   And Stanhope's plans unfold the soul of Pope."

Even as the churchwardens, some sixty years ago,
unfolded the soul of some great master-builder
by breaking down his carved work with axes
and hammers, to make way for galleries and
comfortable family pews.

Horace Walpole bears further testimony to
the degradations of horticulture in his own and
in preceding generations, to the great waste of
money and labour in servile imitation of the
artificial, architectural, and aquatic arrangements
which had been introduced by the Romans. He
affirms that all the ingredients of Pliny's garden
corresponded exactly with those laid out by

London and Wise, the popular landscape gardeners of the day: the same shrubs methodically trimmed, the same pipes spouting water, the same straight walks with hedges of box, the same long lines in alternation of obelisks and trees. There were castles, and beasts, and birds, clipped out of evergreen shrubs, including a triumphal achievement in the form of a " wren's nest, that was capacious enough to receive a man upon a seat provided for his comfort." The venerable oak, the romantic beech, the useful elm, even the aspiring circuit of the lime, the regular round of the chestnut, the almost moulded orange, were fantastically shaped by the shears. Terraces were raised, with stone steps, and heavy balustrades; and there were cloisters, arched and paved, and covered with roofs of lead.

Sir William Temple, although he thoroughly appreciated the fresh air, the verdure, and the fragrance of a garden, and spoke of horticulture as being not only the inclination of kings, and the choice of philosophers, but as the common favourite of public and private men, a pleasure of the greatest, and the care of the meanest,

E

an employment and possession for which no man is too high or too low; yet could not emancipate himself from the conventional delusions of his day, from admiration of straight walks on gravel, 300 paces in length, and broad in proportion, bordered by standard laurels stationed at intervals, like policemen lining a street for a procession; of the large parterre, divided into quarters by more gravel walks; of grottoes, embellished with figures of shell rockwork; of summer-houses, stone stairs, statues, and water-works, in profusion. "I will not enter into any account of flowers," he writes, "having only pleased myself with seeing or smelling them, and not troubled myself with the care, which is more the ladies' part than the men's; but the success is wholly in the gardener." He was, notwithstanding, like a baby "beginning to take notice," when he qualified his eulogia of walls and water with the words—"What I have said of the best forms of gardens is meant only of such as are in some sort regular; for there be many other forms, wholly irregular, that may, for aught I know, have more beauty than any of the others; but they must owe it to some extraordinary disposition of Nature, or some great race of fancy, or judgment in the contrivance, which may produce many disagreeing parts into some figure, which shall yet upon the whole be very agreeable." And he was again illuminated when he affirmed that he knew not three wiser precepts for the conduct either of princes or private than these,

> " Servare modum, finemque tueri,
> *Naturamque sequi* " ;

but his heart was not with the flowers but with the fruits, and in their culture he had great success, importing new varieties, and improving the old.

There were other men of renown, at the time of Queen Anne, and near it, who reverently admired the natural world around them,

> " By suffering worn and weary,
> But beautiful as some fair angel still,"

with a special worship for their gardens, such as were Evelyn of Wooton, the author of " Sylva," a discourse on forest trees, and Gilbert White, who wrote the history of his birthplace, Selborne ; but the triumvirate whom we gardeners, who love the natural or English system, most delight to honour are Pope, Addison, and Walpole. I have placed them in order of merit, and disclaiming all allegiance to the Bishop of Rome, I boldly maintain the Supremacy of a Pope. He was *facile princeps.* He not only denounced, with brilliant satire and irresistible common sense, that which was false in principle, and therefore feeble in result, but he set before his contemporaries as an object-lesson, which he had learned from an Omniscient Teacher, that which was always true and beautiful. He did more than this; and, because the witnesses of his success on the banks of the Thames were few, and the loggerheads who derided his scheme were many, he instigated and instructed others, and sent them forth as missionaries among the heathen.

Should the Royal Horticultural Society ever erect a Walhalla, the most prominent statue must be that of Pope — a bust, perhaps, in preference to a full figure, seeing that his anatomical arrangements were so irregular that, associated with a spirit of insatiable inquiry, they suggested his resemblance to a note of interrogation, a little crooked thing which asks questions.

Pope found a man after his own heart, a man dear to the heart of every true gardener, in Kent. London and Wise were for some time the favourite landscape-gardeners of the fashionable world, although their gardens had little to do with landscapes. They adhered to the Italian system of geometrical beds with box edgings, with embellishments of black earth and white and yellow sand.

Charles the Second imported Le Notre with a few of his French friends, but, with great abilities and splendid opportunities, he followed the old lines. They excelled in formal design and construction, but it had not as yet occurred to them that the Creator had set a model before them infinitely more beautiful than their own imaginations. Le Notre, who insisted upon two arrangements which were in opposition to nature, namely, that the garden should in every way differ from its surroundings, and that all beds and trees should have duplicates so as to " balance " each other, disfigured the grand old château at Fontainebleau with avenues of cropped limes, and King Charles might as well have invited Tournefort, who denied the sexes of the plants, to come over and teach us botany. A Frenchman of to-day would say to us, *nous avons changé tout cela*, and would take us to the Bois de Boulogne.

It was said of Kent that he leapt the fence and saw that all nature was a garden, but the metaphor was not felicitous, because his predecessor Bridgeman had *sunk* the *fence* altogether, and therefore there was nothing to leap. Bridgeman invented one of the most simple and at the same time most charming of all our adjuncts to a garden, by removing the soil at the boundary, making a wall of sufficient height to sustain the earth and keep out the cattle, and then by a gradual slope returning to the original level. This arrangement, when carefully made, is imperceptible in the distance, and comes upon the stranger with such a sudden surprise, that he is supposed to utter, in an ecstasy of admiration, the " Ha-Ha " which gave the barrier its name. In numberless examples (my old home in Nottinghamshire is one) this substitution of a fair view, of the free and open country, in place of a brick wall has been almost as great a revelation as when the curtain is withdrawn from a picture, or the sun shines after a shower.

Bridgeman must have a nook in the Walhalla, but he was only a herald of the coming man, an aide-de-camp to Field-Marshal Kent.

Kent was a man of exquisite taste and an accomplished artist. He commenced his pictorial career as a coach-painter. The coach in his day was not as in ours a beautiful toy, on which rich noblemen and gentlemen, and a few masculine ladies display their manipulations in "tooling the four spanking tits," while a guard in a tall white hat tantivies on a five-foot horn; it was not only an object of admiration as a work of genius, but as the only vehicle by which the king's lieges could be conveyed with marvellous rapidity through the length and breadth of the land. Nevertheless it failed to satisfy Kent's ambitions with regard to decorative art, and he made such successful progress that on his return from Italy, where he had been sent to study, he produced many excellent pictures of historical subjects with which some of our great mansions, such as Stowe and Burlington House, were adorned on ceiling and wall.

He was an architect also, but he was designed for better things than these. He was to paint with colours which were never seen upon a palette, he was to raise structures which no builder could plan. It was

> " Kent who felt
> The pencil's power, but fired with higher forms
> Of beauty than that pencil knew to paint,
> Worked with the living hues, which Nature lent,
> And realised his landscapes."

He loved Art much, but he loved Nature more; and he rejoiced to find in the formation and culture of a garden, in the selection, disposition, combination, and contrast of trees, shrubs, and flowers, their beautiful co-operation. Nature teaching and Art eager to learn, Nature in command and Art in reverent admiration with goodwill doing service. Writers and gardeners had long been harassed by uncomfortable con-jectures that their horticulture might be im-proved, but they satisfied themselves with drowsy dreams and sterile intentions, and fol-lowed each other on the old Roman roads like a procession of Pickford's vans, copying the old patterns of straight walks and geometrical beds, still retaining the mossy statues with no features to speak of and no limb that could be warranted sound, fearless as to the exhalations of stagnant pools, sharpening the ancestral garden shears, and clipping caricature peacocks out of huge masses of yew and box. It was reserved for Bacon and Walpole, Addison, Pope, Wheatley, Mason the poet, and others to condemn the rigid formalities, the monotonous repetitions, the ostentation, the incongruity of the Italian system, and by rhyme and by reason, in poetry and prose, with scathing satire and simple argument, to originate a reformation. Pope seems to have been the first who proved by visible illustrations the truth of his principles, and Kent, instructed, it is said, by his precepts, and informed by his example, with the consummate taste of an artist, the zeal of an enthusiast, and the practical knowledge of a landscape gardener, gradually introduced and established the English or natural system.

What does this mean? It means, briefly, a collection of the most beautiful trees, shrubs, and flowers which you can procure for the space at your disposal, so arranged and tended that they may seem indigenous, and happy in their homes, each to be admired for its individual merits, and mutually enhancing the charms of its neighbour by contrast or by combination; but this subject must be discussed in detail.

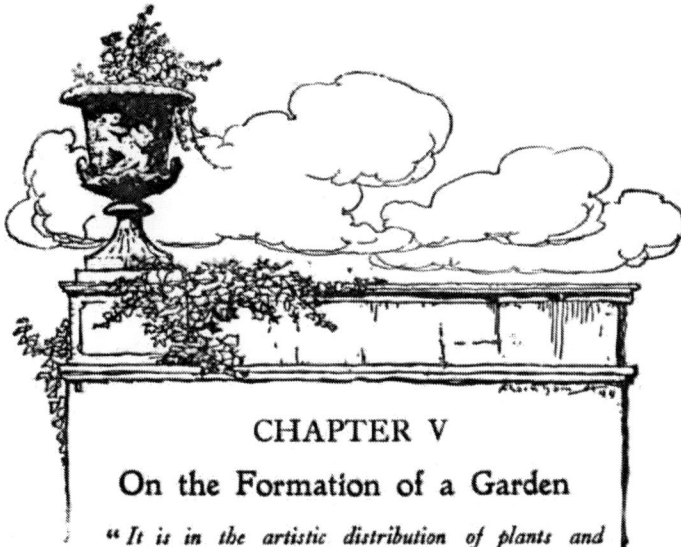

CHAPTER V

On the Formation of a Garden

"It is in the artistic distribution of plants and groups, so as to do away with continuity of lines, and to blend each individual object with all the rest, that the highest power of a garden will consist, and the greatest praise which could be bestowed on any design, would be, that its various parts seemed to fit into their proper places, and to harmonise with each other."—KEMP.

HOW far are architecture and horticulture compatible? Should there be terraces, balustrades, stone-edgings, steps, vases, and urns?

Years ago, I had a neighbour and friend in Nottinghamshire, who was also one of my rivals at our local flower-shows. Propelled by an

inquisitive spirit beyond the boundaries of eti-
quette and good taste, he "happened to be
passing my home," but a short time before an
exhibition, at which we were to compete for a
silver cup, to be given to the best collection of
calceolarias in pots, and "thought he would just
look in." Our plants were unusually good, but
the survey did not elicit any note of admiration,
and the surveyor turned to my gardener, and
coolly asked what treatment he proposed to
adopt in the interval before the show? My
prime minister, who held office for half a century
at Caunton Manor, a shrewd Yorkshireman, full
of wise experience—he must have been very full,
for no scrap ever escaped him—was dumb awhile
in surprise and indignation,

> "A moment o'er his face
> A tablet of unutterable thoughts was traced,"

and then he said, with all the solemnity of a
foreman communicating to a judge the verdict
of his jury, " *It depends*," and departed.

The same reply is appropriate to the inquiry
as to an alliance between the builder and the
gardener—"it depends." The palatial residence,

(which is auctioneer for palace), the castle with its cloud-capped towers, the great mansion on the hill, suggest a terrace, as a modification of their size, a relief from their uniformity, a beautiful carpet spread before a stately throne, the representative of Art coming forth to do homage to Nature, or as a delightful promenade from which we may admire them both.

On either side of this walk, which may be either of gravel or stones, there may be broad borders of grass, oft mown and rolled, with flower-beds of a rational form at intervals, and edged with stone. The wall outside the terrace should be covered with climbing plants, growing out of a bed, not too wide, of herbaceous or half-hardy plants—the latter to be preferred, where the supplies are abundant, inasmuch as they may be preceded by the flowers of spring, and followed (though this experiment is seldom satisfactory) by a winter-garden. Beyond this may be further descents by stone stairs to terrace walks, with more beds and vases for flowers, fountains, and statues, until the boundary is reached, whether it be a low wall or sunk fence.

Here the architect and the gardener should lift their hats and take leave of each other, with the mutual understanding that the works which they had done in conjunction is no more the garden than the balustrades and the steps, the water-works, and the sculptures, are the house. It is ornamental ground, "dressed ground," as it is sometimes designated, and as such is in many instances greatly to be admired, but *it is not the garden*, and the term, too often applied, is a misnomer.

The accomplished architect is a benefactor to mankind. He adorns our lands, and he gladdens our life, with the beauty and comfort of our homes. Nowhere is his graceful art more abundantly displayed than in our own country, in our cathedrals and churches, our colleges, our halls and habitations.

> " The stately homes of England,
>   How beautiful they stand,
>   Amidst their tall ancestral trees
>   O'er all the pleasant land !
>   The deer across their greensward bound,
>   Through shade and sunny gleam,
>   And the swan glides past them with the sound
>   Of some rejoicing stream ! "

But beyond the precincts to which I have referred we do not require his service.

There was a time when the architect was an obtrusive and persistent poacher; when, not content with his edifices of brick and stone, his terraces, pagodas, colonnades, and cupolas, urns and tubs in front of his houses, he insisted on a repetition of walls, towers, domes, and spires done elsewhere in evergreen shrubs; and when it was written by one of the brotherhood that he should not trouble his readers with any curious rules for shaping and fashioning of a garden or orchard, how long, broad, or high the beds, hedges, or borders should be contrived, *every drawer, embroiderer, nay almost every dancing-master, may pretend to such niceties,* in regard that they call for very small invention and less learning. *Now* we shall be justified in associating such an utterance with "an out-patient of a lunatic asylum" (the description given to me many years ago, by a sarcastic rural policeman, of a neighbour whom he despised), but *then,* when the gardeners themselves followed the same straight lines in their walks, copied the same fantastic forms in their knots and beds, which squirmed and wriggled like the poor worms pricked by the hook, when they mutilated vegetation, and gloried in their shame, there was too much truth in the satire. The garden was regarded as a mere appendage to the house, and it was a condescension and work of supererogation on the part of the architect to superintend its formation.

The idea of superiority is not extinct. I have heard complaints from builders that we gardeners trespass upon their work, and disfigure it with our ampelopsis, wistaria, jasmine, roses, and ivy; but no one outside their fraternity seconds the proposition. Has not the Great Architect of the Universe clothed His mountains and rocks with moss, and lichen, and flowers? And yet within a few years an architect has informed us that a garden should be laid out in an equal number of rectangular parts; that everything therein should be simple, formal, and *logical!* and that he should have no more hesitation in applying the scissors to his trees and shrubs with a view to their transformation into pyramids and peacocks, cocked hats and ramping lions, than he should experience in mowing his grass.

Should this gentleman secure the sympathy of the public with his rectifications of Nature, it will only remain for the Government to invite contracts for the fulfilment of the Quaker's suggestion that the world should be painted a good, cheap, universal drab.

Meanwhile we may be permitted to consider the formation and contents of a garden. There are no hard and fast definitions, no designs in stereotype, for a garden. The space, the site, the surroundings, the soil, are so diverse, that you might as well ask a physician to prescribe without a diagnosis, or an architect to build without a specification, as invite an expert to design, or to improve, a garden without a survey of the ground. There are persons who would undertake, on the receipt of a photograph, to supply every defect and make you beautiful for ever, but they are not gardeners.

There are laws, nevertheless, immutable as those of the Medes and Persians, of universal application, everywhere and always to be obeyed. There must be in every garden—

The grace of *Congruity*. There must be unity without uniformity, a pleasing combination not

F

only of the separate parts of the garden, but of the garden itself with the scene around. Every instrument in the great orchestra must be in tune.

Le Notre, who for a time had a great reputation in France and England as a landscape gardener, was deceived by the fond hallucination that a garden should be formed in the most distinct antagonism and the most striking contrast to the general aspect of the land. If situated among mountains, it must be as flat as the walls of Jericho; if on the plain, there must be mounds and embankments. Nature must really be put "in form." She was too short, and too small, and she must be padded, and must wear the highest of heels, and the tallest of hats and plumes. She was too tall, and must be asked to sit down. But Nature does not acquiesce. She will accept the respectful service of the neat-handed Phyllis with her brushes and combs, but she declines to wear other people's hair. She loves the pure water in the marble bath, but she despises the dyes and the paints. You may rectify, arrange, develop, or alas you may disfigure and destroy; but if you would win the approbation of her smile, you will never think to thwart her, and only to alter or assist, as she may teach you; ever listening for her instructions, and obeying the intimations which she gives.

I have watched with great interest attempts to improve Nature. I remember an under-gardener, who carved flowers with his pocket-knife out of turnips, chiefly the ranunculus, the camellia, and the tulip, and coloured them with stripes and spots of the most gorgeous hues; and I recall a day when, passing by the potting-shed, in which he was exhibiting his splendid achievements to a friend, I heard him say, "They whacks natur'—don't they, Dobbs?" And Dobbs replied, "They whacks her ea-sy."

On another occasion, in my undergraduate days, I was with a brother Oxonian in the suburbs of London, and in a tea-garden attached to a public-house we saw a gigantic palm-tree, made from cast iron, and vividly painted green and gold. My companion, a young gentleman of infinite jest and irrepressible mirth, entered the enclosure, and in the presence of the pro-prietor began to express his admiration of the tree, as though it were a grand reality in all the vigour of its growth. This he did with a

grave enthusiasm, which made me ache with
suppressed emotion, and which so delighted the
publican that he favoured us with records of his
personal history, informing us that he was an
Italian, had been a waiter at Monte Carlo, had
kept a Pension at Bordighera, and that he loved
La Palma; but when, tapping the trunk of the
tree, and eliciting sounds which were decidedly
metallic, my companion proceeded to make
inquiries as to the quantity and quality of the
dates, with an offer to purchase a small quantity
for an invalid uncle in Norfolk (invalid uncle
in Norfolk composed on the spot), I noticed a
sudden change in the countenance of our host,
and took prompt measures to avert an explosion
by the application of my elbow to the ribs of my
friend, and by an adroit order for refreshment.

Congruity means the adaptation of Art to
Nature, the conformity of a garden with its
environs, the study of the soil—

> "Et quid quæque ferat regio, quid quæque recuset."

It means not only the selection but the setting
of the jewels, not only the painting of the
picture, but the placing in the frame.

The transition from horticulture to agriculture should be gradual, through the wild garden to the open field, from the lawn to the park, from the park to the scene beyond, and it has been suggested accordingly that,

> " To make the landscape grateful to the sight,
>   Three points of distance always should unite ;
>   And, howsoe'er the view may be confined,
>   Three marked divisions we shall always find."

This study of the *tout ensemble* is a first principle of landscape gardening. Mr. Robert Marnock was the champion of the English or natural system, and was the most accomplished artist we have had in the design or the development of a garden. He had not that great constructive genius which won for Paxton so much honour—knighthood, a place in Parliament, the admiration of his countrymen, and of multitudes who came from all parts of the world in 1851, to see our great Exhibition (who that saw does not remember with delight his first entrance into that lovely palace of Art, as a thing of beauty and a joy for ever, with the birds singing in the great green trees, and everywhere sweet music and bright hues ?)—nor has he

left us such valuable literary contributions as
Paxton's Botanical Dictionary, Flower Garden,
and Magazine; but among our landscape gardeners—and I write with full appreciation of good
work done by Thomas, Milner, and others—
he was *facile princeps*. He kindly came to my
little garden in Nottinghamshire to give me
advice as a brother and a friend. He was
indeed the brother born for adversity, for I
was at that time, as a gardener, in a state of
extreme prostration and debility from a simultaneous attack of scarlet and yellow fever. In
the first delirium of the disease, which went
by the name of " Bedding-out," and declared
itself in profuse eruptions of every colour and
form, I committed enormities which would have
justified a commission *de lunatico inquirendo*. I
felled trees, I removed shrubberies, I levelled
undulations, I swept away nooks and corners,
for my grand display of half hardy plants.
For some six summers the symptoms annually
returned: then gradually my temperature went
down to normal. My reason was restored, and my
aching eyes turned away from their kaleidoscope.
I date my recovery from a certain morning in

July. On the preceding day my floral fireworks were in their most perfect splendour, with circles of gold (*Calceolaria*), scarlet (*Geranium*), silver (*Centaurea*), bronze (*Perilla*), purple (*Verbena*), blue (*Lobelia*), and grey (*Ageratum*). I was expecting in a few hours a large garden-party, the *élite* of the neighbourhood. I rose early and looked out of the window. There had been a thunderstorm and a tempest, with drenching rains. The appearance was more like a palette than a picture. Only the Perillas seemed to realise the situation, for they looked like the feathers on a hearse.

I awoke, but the lawn, and the almonds, and the mespilus, and the cistus, the laburnums and the lilacs, where were they? I resolved to complete that which the storm had suggested; to apply the sponge to the slate; and on my *tabula rasa* to delineate and realise another plan. Three friends, three famous friends—Mr. Robert Marnock aforesaid, Mr. William Robinson, and Mr. William Ingram, who had established at Belvoir the most beautiful spring garden in Europe—came to give me not advice merely, but personal, practical help. They had known me in better circumstances, when, as a virtuous young gardener, I kept the even tenor of my way upon the ancient roads of sobriety, contentment, and common sense. They remembered me before my palate was vitiated by lobsters, cayenne pepper, and grills; before my eyes were dazed by coruscations; before I behaved like some foolish insect, who turns its back on the security and sweetness of the garden for the open window of the brilliant salon, and scorches its wings at the lamp.

They revived my hopes. They showed possibilities. They assured me that the erubescence, shingles, jaundice, and eczema would yield to treatment, cooling medicines, and simpler food. Dr. Marnock, physician in ordinary to Queen Flora, would take a diagnosis and would send a prescription. I recall his massive figure and intellectual face as he stood alone, like Marius at Carthage, or like the engravings we so often see of the great Bonaparte (frivolously described by the profane jester as "Napoleon out at elbow") examining his patient. He made a long investigation, moving slowly from place to place, and writing brief memoranda in his notebook. He told me that his first desire was to preserve every scrap of existing vegetation which was worth keeping, then to consider what accessories should be made, and then to blend them together, as gracefully and naturally as his knowledge and his love should teach—like the wise householder who brings out of his treasures things new and old. He told me very little of that which he proposed to do, but it was more than enough to hear that "he thought he saw what would please." Then he sent a most intelligent foreman to complete his design, and in a few short years he "made the desert smile." There was not a straight walk, nor a straight line, nor an angle in his plan; there were no stars and garters. There were no lanky standards, wobbling like overgrown giants in various stages of decay.

Watching this transformation with a supreme felicity, I gradually forgot the horrors of the Revolution, only reminded now and then, when indigestion produced among my visions of the night a huge octopus (once the *chef de'œuvre* of my bedding-out) crawling with tentacles about nine feet long to clasp and crush me.

There were no *incongruities*. I have spoken
of unseemly intrusions upon horticulture by
the mason with his bricks, by the plumber
with his leaden pipes, by the barber with his
shears.   There still remain sad examples of
"unsubstantial tawdriness" (Walpole), walks
of powdered bricks and slates, cockles, and
coloured sands.   We had an arbour in our
childhood of birch lined with moss, and floored
with squares of flat tiles and sheep's trotters in
alternation.   Tubs, so highly respectable in their
own sphere of usefulness, where we wash clothes
and brew beer, fail to charm as receptacles for
trees.   The poets do not make them a theme
of song, and they are not found in the picture
galleries.   The trees themselves, equidistant on
either side of a walk, seem to ask our compassion, and we almost hear them sighing, "We
don't know what we've done."

"The Hermit's Cell" is alike deplorable.
The Hermit in sackcloth; an old worn-out bag
with the letters "Brown & Co., maltsters," faintly
legible, on his back.   He was supposed to be
occupied in devotion, but he did not look devo-
tional, closely resembling the prints of "Fagin in

Prison," and leaving a strong impression upon the mind of the spectator, that he was capable of any crime. Imagine our childish ecstasy, when a pair of robins built their nest in his beard, originally of snowy wool, but

"Qui color, albus erat nunc est contrarius albo,"

and brought up a family under his very nose.

Aviaries are interesting, where the guano is occasionally removed, and when the inhabitants are not engaged in fighting or moulting; but *give me the dear birds in their freedom.*

This then should be the primary endeavour of the true gardener, to collect all the most beautiful specimens which he can obtain of trees, and shrubs, and flowers, and to arrange them with all the knowledge which he possesses of their habit, colour, and form, in accordance with the simplicity, the graceful outlines, the charming combinations of the natural world beyond,

"Where order in variety we see,
And where, though all things differ, all agree."

Working under these rules, copying this model, obeying Pope's edict,

"First follow Nature, and your judgment frame
By her just standard, which is still the same,"

he will make but few mistakes, and these will
suggest their own rectification, whereas all the
endeavours of wealth and self-conceit to follow
their own imaginations, without regard to these
immutable laws, and to obtain the admiration
of their neighbours by the mere costliness of
their novelties, or the heterogeneous location of
their plants, inevitably fail. Again and again
I have seen such results of lavish expenditure
and stolid arrogance as have almost induced
ophthalmia and softening of the brain, with an
intense longing for the wings of a dove; whereas the same eyes have gazed with a delight,
which could not tire, in many a garden where
the means were scanty, but the love was large.

Of course there must be *Variety*. It might
be inferred from an inspection of the majority
of our gardens, that no novelty had been introduced into this country for the last sixty or
seventy years, and that straight walks through
huge clumps of evergreens (chiefly laurels) and
their boundless continuity of shade left nothing to
be desired. The true gardener will thankfully
avail himself of all the beneficent gifts which
reward his patient study and science in the pro-

duction of new varieties. When we old gentlemen walk through the tents of the great Flower
Show in the Temple Gardens, and, remembering
the orchids, the roses, the lilies, the narcissus,
the clematis, the carnations of sixty years ago,
contrast the present with the past, we are
astonished not only by the marvellous progress
which has been made, but by the foreknowledge
that in another fifty years nearly all that is before
us will be superseded. There may be a momentary shadow of regret upon our spirit, for the
favourites which we have lost and for those
which will soon be gone, but it fades when
we think of all the joy which they have
brought, and of all the happiness in store for
our children's children.

In every garden there must be, wherever there
may be, *Seclusion*, quiet retreats for rest and re-
tirement, for contemplation made. Our garden
should be our Jerusalem, "the vision and possession of Peace." I must have a place to flee
unto, when I know that the great landau of the
Wopperton-Wickses is on my avenue, because one
of their gigantic horses, a little touched in the
wind, is loudly expressing his disapproval of a

sudden rise in the ground, and because I catch a
glimpse through the trees of the gorgeous liveries,
the cockades, and the calves, and the elaborate
armorial bearings of the Woppertons and the
Wickses mixed.

I am fond of my fellow-men. I am a gregari-
ous and not a solitary snipe, I do not attempt to
justify the notorious custom of certain country
squires, to rush into their shrubberies like rabbits
by a covert side on the approach of visitors;
but there are a few persons, querulous tattlers,
accusers of the brethren with harsh voices, which
startle one with a sudden horror, like the trom-
bone player in the village band who spoiled their
chief performance at the "Penny Reading," by a
sudden note of terrible discord which made the
whole audience jump. Asked for an explanation
by his indignant leader, he replied, "I came
all at once on a note as I'd never met afore, and
I hadn't time to see as it wor only a fly-mark,
and so I played un."

It is from these dissonant intrusions which
confuse the brain, impede the digestive organs,
and turn the tranquil waters into seething billows,
like the storms of an Italian lake, that we would

provide our haven of refuge. I would not make a single garden which was worth seeing into "a place of selfish solitude." There is rarely need to ask the question now,

> "Why should not these great squires
> Give up their parks some dozen times a year
> And let the people breathe ? "

As a rule, wherever decent behaviour can be assured, the most attractive of our English homes are open to the public. At frequent intervals the true gardener is never more happy than when he has the time for converse with those who can appreciate his work. What I mean is that all gardens should be secluded from supervision, and I think that even on show days there should be some small sanctuary unpolluted by the bag of the sandwich, the peel of the orange, and the cork of the ginger-beer.

Of course in horticulture, as in every other culture, the success depends on the *cultor*. It is not given to him, who has a garden because his father had a garden, and who wishes it to be "kept up" exactly as he found it. It is not given to him who regards all the work of his vocation as something which must be done, and sees little difference between collecting vegetables for the kitchen and cutting flowers for "the rooms." It is given only to the enthusiasm which does not say "I wish" but "I will"—to the patient, devoted service which never ceases to contend with difficulties, insect and weed, drought and frost. It is given to the zeal which sends scores of the artisans of Nottingham to their tiny plots and miniature greenhouses, half a mile away from the town, before and after their daily work, and sometimes at midday in the dinner hours, and which impels my lord and lady to leave the beau-monde of London society in the height of the season because "we must have a look at the garden." It is a pure and steadfast homage which abides for ever in the heart where it has found a home. *Cælum non animum mutat* —it goes with us to every clime.

Hear the pathetic testimony of one who went "with Kitchener to Khartoum," and after the great victory of Omdurman to the last earthly home of the Soldier Saint: "In the garden you somehow came to know Gordon, and to feel near to him. Here was an Englishman doing his duty, alone and at the instant peril of *his life;*

yet still he loved his garden. The garden was a yet more pathetic vision than the palace. The palace accepted its doom mutely; the garden strove against it. Untrimmed, unwatered, the oranges and citrons still struggled to bear their little hard green knobs, as if they had been full ripe fruit. The pomegranates put out their vermilion star-flowers, but the fruit was small and woody and juiceless. The figs bore better, but they too were small and without vigour. Rankly overgrown with dhurra, a vine still trailed over a low roof its pale leaves and limp tendrils, but yielded not a sign of grapes. It was all green, and so far vivid and refreshing after Omdurman. But it was the green of nature, not of cultivation; leaves grew large, and fruit grew small and dwindled away. Reluctantly, despairingly, Gordon's garden was dropping back to wilderness. And in the middle of the defeated fruit-trees grew rankly the hateful Sodom apple, the poisonous herald of desolation."

CHAPTER VI

The Component Parts of a Garden

"In the royal ordering of gardens there ought to be gardens for all the months of the year."—LORD BACON.

"Flowers from all heavens, and lovelier than their names,
Grew side by side."

—LORD TENNYSON

FROM the elementary principles we pass to the practical details which should instruct our love of a garden, and our charity begins at home with those climbing plants which beautify the houses in which we live. Not the most admirable, but the most available for every variety of dwelling, great or small, in town or country, is the *Ampelopsis Veitchii*, the greatest to my mind of the many treasures which Mr. Veitch has introduced into this country, because its enjoyment is not restricted to the rich, but is within the means of all who desire it.   On the castle or the cottage it is a charming adornment, self-supporting, requiring neither wire nor nail. That it should be described as " *Vitis inconstans* " is " one of those things no fellow can understand." It is a vine undoubtedly, but it is perfectly hardy, vigorous, and abundant, although not fruitful, upon the walls of thine house.   It may not be so splendid in its colours or so graceful in its form as the dear old Virginian creeper, but it is much more easily managed and is more regular and reliable in its growth.   There are several varieties as to form and tint, but all are pleasing, and their power of transformation upon a gaunt, ugly building, in two or three years with verdure clad, is wonderful.   Some maintain, builders more especially, that good architecture is disfigured by these additions, but I have not met with an example.

Regarding the greatest happiness of the greatest number as the most laudable ambition of benevolent men, I should commend *Clematis Montana* as being one of the most available for general use of our mural decorations, in flower and foliage so fresh and fair. *Jackmanni* and some of the lovely white and lilac varieties should be grown, but they are more difficult as to cultivation, and I prefer them on poles in shrubberies, beds, or borders.

Wistaria sinensis, planted upon a sunny wall, must gladden our eyes in May with its long lilac racemes, and its young leafage of vivid green. It should have ample room, for when it has taken root it covers a large frontage. Sometimes, like a singer after the encores at a concert, the Wistaria gives us, in acknowledgment of our admiration, a second bloom, a most welcome aftermath, a gleaning of the grapes of Ephraim. On a verandah or pergola it has a delightful effect, when carefully tended and trained.

The most imposing plant which grows upon our walls is the *Magnolia* (*magnifolia et grandiflora*), with its great glossy leaves, its buds as large as goblets, and its flowers as white as china bowls. We all know the story of the gentleman who called upon some friends at Mentone, placed his walking-stick made from wood of the Magnolia in a flower-bed adjoining the house,

CLIMBING PLANTS AT GREAT LANGLEY

forgot it, and returning twelve months afterwards found a large party having tea under its
branches.   In this country we are more inclined
to exaggerate its sterility, and in countless cases
the hope of possession is abandoned from want
of confidence in the endurance of the plant or
from failure in its treatment.   With a south-
eastern or southern aspect—the former to be
preferred, because all vegetation rejoices in the
rising of the sun, and in a position where that
chartered libertine the wind does not visit it
too roughly—the Magnolia, with mulching and
matting in its early growth to protect it root
and branch, may be successfully established, and,
with some occasional defence in the future from
bitter and continuous frost, may be securely
preserved.   These coverings are unsightly, but *il
faut soufrir pour être belle*, men must shave and
women must make their toilette; and though as
a rule I strongly object to the introduction of
plants into our gardens, which succumb to the
severities of our climate, and which seem to
apologise with a sickly smile for their unwholesome appearance (*morituri te salutant*), there are
exceptions, as in the present instance, with such

possibilities of reward from perseverance as should
stimulate all our enterprise, even though it begin
with failure.   I do not believe in riding for a fall,
but he is no sportsman who runs no risk, and
he is no gardener who does not bravely contend
with difficulties, who forgets that the husbandman hath long patience, and that Jonah's gourd,
which delighted him with its instantaneous and
abundant shade, although he had not laboured
neither made it to grow, was withered by a worm
when the morning came.

It must be remembered that in this, as in
many other instances, there is a great recuperative
power in plants, even where the influence of
severe weather seems to have been fatally disastrous to the external growth, especially when
the surface of the ground has been thickly
covered with manure.   When it was my privilege,
nearly forty years ago, to be among the first, if
not the first, of those amateur rosarians who
grew tea-roses extensively, *sub Jove frigido*, in
the open air, I had a bed of three hundred
specimens, which after one of our most rigorous
winters (I think it was in 1860–61) was draped
in solemn black, and all that could be seen was

frozen to death.   My friends and neighbours
regarded them with a rueful countenance, and
made their lamentations, to the best of their
dramatic ability ; but I felt that behind the
mask and within the silence there was joy and
peace, and that as soon as they were out
of my garden they would congratulate each
other on the results of my audacity in an
attempt to grow tea-roses *al fresco*, which they
had always denounced as " utter rot."   Not one
of those rose-trees was dead!   Budded low
on the briar, and enclosed on all sides with
some eight inches of solid farmyard manure,
they came up all the stronger for the pruning
which Jack Frost had applied, and oh, how
thoroughly we all admired, and how surely we
had all foreseen, this most delightful display!

A similar incident occurred to me with one
of the most lovely of our climbing flowers,
which should be seen on every home, *Passiflora
Constance Elliott*.   Making inquiry from a friend,
on whose house I first saw it in its perfect
beauty, with its long trailing festoons of foliage,
and its multitude of flowers bearing the sacred
emblems of the passion, as to the health of his

plant, I was grieved to hear that "it had perished in the winter, and he had dug it up." I went with a sad heart to look at my own belongings. I saw no sign of life, I cleared away the copious mulching, I gently and gradually removed the soil, until I saw to my supreme felicity a small spot, white faintly tinged with green, which assured me of an awaking from the long winter sleep. I replaced the earth as tenderly as a mother would rearrange the coverings of a little child, who had been restless in its crib, and for many summers since, never so profusely as in 1898, it has bloomed on the Deanery walls.

Many trees, shrubs, and flowers, which are established among our hardy favourites, would have been discarded soon after their introduction into our gardens, had their owners been disheartened by their tardy growth, or by their apparent inability to withstand our frosts, before they became acclimatised. Philip Miller, referring in his Gardener's Dictionary to the Laurel, writes: "I know it will be objected that these trees are often destroyed by hard winters, and so are improper to make large plantations in England. That they have been sometimes killed by severe winters I cannot deny; but if they are brought up hardily, and not sheared, I dare affirm they will resist the severest cold of our climate; when grown to a moderate age, provided they are planted in a dry soil, in which, though their leaves should be entirely shrivelled by extreme cold, yet, if permitted to remain undisturbed, and not cut, they will shoot again in the succeeding summer. In the hard winter of 1728 most of these trees were dug up and thrown away as dead, whereas the few which were permitted to remain did shoot out in the succeeding summer and recovered their verdure."

The blue variety *Passiflora cærulea* is beautiful, but so far as my experience goes it is neither so handsome nor so hardy as *Constance Elliott*. *Eccremocarpus scaber* is another gay and graceful climber with bright orange flowers, and is worthily named as *Calampelis*, the Beautiful Vine, which it resembles in its habit of growth. *Garrya Elliptica* is, as Mrs. Earle in her "Pot-pourri from a Surrey Garden" describes it, "a charming evergeen with fascinating catkins."

Two *Jasmines* should be grown on our walls the *White*, beloved from childhood, and the

Yellow, which comes to us in its golden bloom, when all around is desolate, to cheer the ungenial day; two *Cydonias* (the Japanese Quince), the *Red*, our old friend *Pyrus Japonica*, and the *White*, which forms a pretty contrast in contiguity with the red, like a bride, clad in robes of virgin white, by her soldier husband's side; two *Cotoneasters*, *microphylla*, and a much brighter variety, *Simmondsii*; *Ceanothus*, *Gloire de Versailles*, *Cratægus Pyracantha*, evergreen, lovely in leaf and flower, and ever charming, but most of all in its dense clusters of brilliant fruit; the golden and silver leaved *Euonymus*, to be always included; *Bignonia Radicans*, with its gay trumpet flowers; and the *Cheimonanthus Fragrans*, well worthy of its Greek and Latin appellations, as our fragrant winter flower, producing its sweet odours in Christmas-tide, bringing us happy memories of a time that is past, and happy hopes of a time that is to come, in which all the gardens send up their incense to Him whose breath perfumes them, and whose pencil paints.

Of the *Honeysuckles* (*Lonicera*), *Halleana* and *Japonica* are the most charming, and when a variety of the latter, *aureo reticulata*, finds a suitable site and soil, its foliage of green and gold is exquisite.

The common ivy, *Hedera Helix*, although it is a comely concealment for red bricks and other ugly erections, huge and bald, and is also most appropriate for ivy-mantled towers and for ruins,

> "Creeping where no life is seen,
> A rare old plant is the ivy green,"

is somewhat too sombre and monotonous for domestic ornamentation, not to mention the injury which it may do if its roots are not prevented from penetrating the mortar; but some of the golden-leaved and silver-leaved varieties are very attractive.

No millionaire, no marquis, not majesty itself, can persuade *Tropæolum Speciosum* to display upon castle walls the abundant foliage, the brilliant flowers, the blue berries of metallic hue, which in Scotland clothe the shepherd's home—one of many striking examples in which we see the benign law of compensation bestowing upon the poor certain privileges, such as a keen appetite and sound sleep, not always given to the rich

In some instances this "*Flame Nasturtium*"
condescends to flourish in England and Wales, and
therefore every gardener should make the experiment; but as one of many who have often failed,
with seed, with cuttings, with rooted plants, sent
to me from over the Border, I must remind him of
the ancient adage, " Happy are they who expect
nothing, for they shall not be disappointed."

Last in the procession, but in the place of
honour, comes *the Royal Rose*. It may surprise
some to be told that only those who have grown
roses upon walls have seen them in the most
perfect phase of their beauty, but from this
additional warmth and shelter they acquire a
vigour of growth and an abundance of bloom
which they do not attain elsewhere.   This development is most remarkable in the Hybrid Tea
and the tea-scented roses, and some of the most
charming specimens which I have seen, including
the magnificent *Jean Ducher*, which I have never
succeeded in producing elsewhere in its integrity,
have been grown upon a wall.   I should not,
however, select roses for a house from the latter
family, with the exception of such robust varieties
as *Gloire de Dijon, Madame Berard, Reine Marie*

Henriette, and *Reve d'or* (all of which should be grown,) but prefer *Turner's Crimson Rambler*, *Madam Alfred Carriére*, *William Allan Richardson*, the *Banksian*, white and yellow, *Charles Lawson*, and *Blairii* 2 ; and, when a rapid and extensive integument is needed, some of the evergreen hardy climbers, such as *Felicité Perpetué* (the name alone should commend it), *Dundee Rambler*, *Myrianthes*, *Rampant*, and *Ruga*. Planted in good soil, they will grow anywhere, and quickly make their way to the roof.

When we have thus adorned our dwellings, and "there's a rose looking in at the window," what should he see who looks out of it? I have said my say about terraces. With or without them, there should be in front of every home a piece of green grass, as spacious as the means permit, well mown, well rolled, kept free from worm and weed. "The lawn," writes Mr. Robinson, "is the heart of the garden, and the happiest thing that is in it." Flowers may come, and leaves may go, the lawn goes on for ever. It refreshes the spirit through the eye, which never tires. It is most to be admired when it imperceptibly joins a park with its ancient trees, its oaks, elms, beeches, chestnuts, limes, sycamores, cedars, pines, firs, and thorns, sunlit river, and distant view; but is always exhilarating, in the London Square, the College Quadrangle, the small suburban plot. Whether the lawn has been long laid down, or recently formed from sods, or from the seeds of fine grasses specially grown for this purpose, it requires constant supervision to eliminate weeds and to preserve its even surface, but the results will richly repay. The ground should be drained if necessary, and manure—none so good as bone-dust—applied occasionally. It must be copiously watered in time of drought.

We wander all over the world in search of things pleasant to the eye; we find them here and there; but nothing delights us more than the green fields and the green lawns, which are only to be seen at home. "Nothing is more pleasant to the eye," writes Lord Bacon, "than green grass kept finely shorn;" and I have before me a plan of Pope's Garden at Twickenham, drawn by his gardener, and published soon after his death, in which all the space between his house and the river is occupied by the lawn; and in the garden behind, approached by a subterraneous passage under the London and Hampton Road, there is a large bowling-green in addition to the grass-plots.

I ask leave to narrate two episodes appropriate to lawns, having a good hope that they will impart to my readers the same satisfaction which they gave to me.

I. My friend Longfield is a man of large possessions and an enthusiastic gardener. He is the proprietor of a pre-eminent lawn, which has ample room for half-a-dozen tennis courts, with simultaneous croquet and bowls. We were contending in this latter game, when his eldest son, an Oxonian, came to ask him whether he and Billy, his brother, might have "a pitch" on this same Campo Santo for occasional practice, if they would promise not to swipe. Longfield was in the 'Varsity Eleven; he was a member of the Marylebone, Zingari, and Free Forester Clubs; he once got 84 at Lords'; he implicitly believes that the greatness of Engand was achieved and is maintained by her superiority in cricket; but this proposal beat him. A frown of dismay and disgust passed like a shadow over his sunny face, and then he rallied like the brave boxer, and came up smiling. "My son," he said, in solemn tones, and raising his right hand like an orator, "you are indeed a worthy disciple of the famous college, to which we both belong, the great Society of the Brasen Nose, and you were doubtless among the anticipations of the poet Horace, when he wrote about the *æs circa pectus*, which may be briefly translated *cheek;* but if you and Billy put a stump into this lawn, both your names go out of my will." Then he whispered in my ear, "Clean bowled!"

II. A gardener, not far from Rochester, having obtained through the kind influence of his master a more lucrative appointment at a lunatic asylum, came back after a year's absence to visit his benefactor, and standing with him on the lawn, he said, "I suppose, sir, you remember Peggy." "Of course," it was answered; "the two-year-old Exmoor pony we bought at Maidstone fair, and put into the mowing-machine when she was almost unbroken. What battles you had, and what a good bit of stuff she was, when she came to years of discretion." "Ah," replied the gardener, "I used to think that no man ever had or could have such a rampageous job; but

H

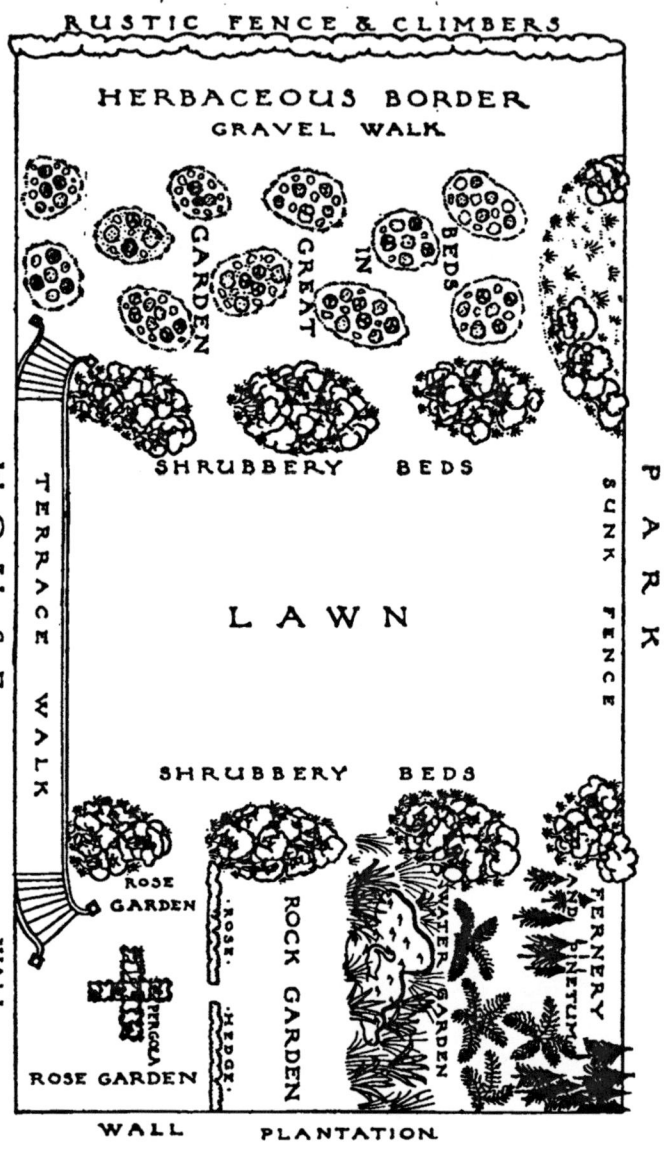

RUSTIC FENCE & CLIMBERS

HERBACEOUS BORDER
GRAVEL WALK

GREAT GARDEN IN BEDS

SHRUBBERY BEDS

HOUSE.

TERRACE WALK

LAWN

WALL

SHRUBBERY BEDS

ROSE GARDEN

PERGOLA

ROSE GARDEN

ROSE. HEDGE.

ROCK GARDEN

WATER GARDEN

FERNERY AND PINETUM

WALL

PLANTATION

PARK

SUNK FENCE

AN IDEAL GARDEN

now that I've got to mow with seven lunatics, *most of 'em wanting to sit down*, I often wish that I was back with Peggy."

The gardens might be placed on either side of the lawn, separated from it by long beds of evergreens and flowering shrubs, either over-lapping each other, with broad spaces of grass between for entrances, or having long intervals for coniferous and other ornamental trees. These beds must be laid out in graceful curves, without points or angles,

> " For Art's unerring rule is only drawn
> From Nature's sacred source,"

and Nature ignores straight lines.

On the east side, supposing the front of the house to have a south aspect, I would place the Great Garden, for the general cultivation of the most beautiful trees, and shrubs, and flowers; and on the west side the smaller gardens for special collections of distinct varieties, such as the Rose Garden, the Rock Garden, the Water Garden, the Fernery, &c.

For the Great Garden I would suggest large round or oval beds (say 30 feet as the diameter

of the circles), and having a circumference of
20 feet of well-kept sward, and whole being
so arranged that there shall be for the visitor
a gradual revelation of beauty, and that the
scene shall continually change.

If the soil of these beds is poor, it must be
enriched, if wet, it must be drained; and then
comes "the selection of the fittest." First of
all, we must bear in mind that we are not pre-
paring a transitory display of perishable plants
which are to bloom for a few weeks,

> " And, like an unsubstantial pageant faded,
>   Leave not a rack behind,"

but that these beds are perennial, and that they
should have their attractions for every season
of the year, being most beautiful, like the rest
of the garden, in the spring and summer, although
they cannot vie in the former with the Alpine
Garden, or, in the latter, with the Herbaceous
Border, and the Rose.

Every group must be the result of thoughtful
study. The true gardener, though he be unable to draw or to paint, must have artistic
admirations and taste. He should be quick to

observe whatsoever things are lovely outside his garden, and these observations should help him in the allocation of his trees and flowers within. "Make that boy copy Nature, not drawings," Flaxman said to the father of John Leech, "and he will be an artist." It is noticeable in those "Collections of Plants, staged for effect," that the most meritorious are those which have the more natural aspect, and so far as this is the case, we may take a hint from them by the substitution of hardy for the more tender varieties of which these groups are composed. You may not have quite the same brillliant hues, but you will have "fast colours, warranted to wash." Not only tints but forms must be regarded. Nature does not turn out her productions, as cooks their jellies, from a mould. She does not plan a clump of poplars in the centre of a plantation, and then gradually diminish her arboretum, until she reaches the ground with a pigmy tree from Japan.

Of course we must expect failures, but they come to teach success; for "Time," it has been well said, "is the best of all gardeners." He not only exposes our mistakes, but shows us how to correct them; and so we bear our disappointments bravely, like the Irishman, who said that his "pig had not weighed so much as he expected, but he never thought it would."

It will be wise, moreover, and will confirm our equanimity if we can fill vacancies, or replace incongruities, from our auxiliary and reserve forces in the private nursery, which should form a part of every large and well-regulated garden.

The supply, from which we may furnish our shrubberies, beds, and borders, is infinite in its extent and variety. Nearly thirty years ago Mr. Mongredien wrote, in his instructive book on "Trees and Shrubs for English Plantations," "Few know, whilst all might and ought to know, that there are 600 trees of surpassing beauty, each pre-eminent for various merits of its own, as regards foliage, flower, fruit, aspect, &c., that will grow in this country in the open air"; and now it is announced in the catalogue of one of our great Hertfordshire nurserymen that his collection contains upwards of 1000 species and varieties. Within my own lifetime there have been introduced into this country, and into my own garden, such treasures as—

Abies.—Cephalonica, Douglasii, Menziesii.

Picea.—Amabilis, Grandis, Lowii, Nobilis, Nordmanniana Pinsapo.

Pinus.—Austriania, Benthamiani, Excelsa, Insignis, Macrocarpa.

Acer.—Several charming varieties, including the Japanese, the *Negundo variegata*, and the *Pseudo Platinus atropurpurea.*

Æsculus rubicunda.—The Scarlet Horse-Chestnut.

Ampelopsis Veitchii.

Aralias.—Japonica and Sieboldii.

Berberis.—Darwinii and others.

Ceanothus.—Gloire de Versailles.

Cedrus.—Atlantica and Deodara.

Cotoneaster.—Microphylla and Simondsii.

Cratægus.—Paul's Scarlet Thorn.

Cryptomeria.—Japonica.

Cupressus.—Lawsoniana.

Desfontania.—Spinosa.

Deutzias.

Escallonias.

Euonymus.

Forsythia viridissima.

Garrya Elliptica.

Hydrangea paniculata grandiflora.

Indigofera.

Jasmenum.—Nudiflorum.

Lonicera.—Japonica.

Mahonias.

Olearia Hasatii.

Osmanthus.

Paulownia.

Pernettia.

Prunus Pissardi.—The lovely cherries, the Japanese and

the double-flowered varieties, *vulgaris* and *sylvestris flore pleno*, are included in the family of Prunus.

Pyrus.—Aria, the white beam-tree, *Aucuparia*, the Mountain Ash, *Malus floribunda*, and a great number of Crabs, alike beautiful in their flowers and fruits, are classified as Pyrus.

Retinosporas.

Rhododendrons.—The Himalayan.

Ribes.

Sequoia.

Skimmias.—Japonica.

Spiræas.

Thujas.

Viburnum.

Weigelas.

All these are common now, and admired throughout the land, but not one of them was in it at the time of my birth, when George the Third was king, and when the beloved lady who now reigns in his stead had not begun to take walking exercise. In our gardens, as everywhere else, "the old order changeth, and giveth place to the new," and there is in horticulture and its importations a signal fulfilment of the ancient prophecy, "Men shall run to and fro, and knowledge shall be increased."

As to plants and flowers, the introductions from our collectors to which I have just referred, the new varieties raised from seed by "cross-fertilisation," the industrial skill of our gardeners, the increase of horticultural shows, the cheapness of wood and glass, have filled the stove, the green-house, and the border with glorious developments of colour and of form.   I recall a time when you might almost have counted on your fingers the orchids of a county, and these in the last stage of galloping consumption.   Happy days for the mealy bug and the red spider, and all manner of flies, under the shade of the tiny panes dis-coloured by dirt and damp, with peaceful homes in the decaying rafters and beams, and warmed by the smoky flue.   In many gardens the sole representative of the Narcissus community was the "Daffydowndilly"; of the Lilies, Candidum; and the Roses, with the exception of the Provence "Cabbage," the Yellow Provence (which as a rule declined to bloom), the miniature Provence, "De Meaux," the Moss Rose, the York and Lancaster, and a few others, which still bloom in ancient gardens, are only known to us through the pages of Mrs. Gore,[1] and the fascinating pictures of Redouté.[2]

---

[1] "The Rose-Fancier's Manual," by Mrs. Gore, 1838.
[2] *Les Roses*, par J. R. Redouté, 1817.

The difficulty of selection in our day arises from an *embarras de richesses*, unknown to our forefathers; but I have carefully prepared the following list, after many years of observation, and in many gardens, from the Land's End to the Border. I could have made large additions to my catalogue, but I preferred experience to hearsay, and I have suffered so much from the "quite hardy" of those whose wish was father to the thought, that I am moved by a compassion for others which personally I have not received.

A LIST OF TREES, SHRUBS, Etc.,

FOR BEDS AND BORDERS

D. deciduous ; *E.* evergreen ; *F.* flowering.

Acacia or *Robinia*, *D.F.*—Described by some as "not perfectly hardy"; but I have grown the old variety *Robinia pseudo-Acacia* for many years in Nottinghamshire, where it has flowered freely, and also *R. Hispiaa*, the *Rose Acacia*. The latter is of dwarf and straggling habit, but the flowers are beautiful.

Acer (Maple), *D.*, suggests sweet associations to those who have enjoyed its syrup in the States, and it delights our eyes at home with many and diverse charms. Of these I would specially commend *Pseuao-Platinus atro-purpureum*, for the rich colours of its leaves; *Lutescens,* for its golden glory in the spring; *Negundo variegatum,* bright in silvery sheen, and a pretty contrast with its neighbours in the shrubbery, especially with its cousins from Japan, the purple and red varieties of *Acer palmatum polymorphum.* These strangers are somewhat shy, and require a little protection, with as much sun as they can get; but I believe that they will become acclimatised, and all gardeners should give them a trial.

Amorpha (False Indigo), *D.F.*—An undergraduate would translate this "not in form," but it is a pretty shrub, with an abundance of purple flowers, and the leaves of *Canescens* are hoar, though not with age.

Amygladus (Almond), *D.F.*—To me the most exhilarating of all the early harbingers of spring; as Spenser wrote—

> " With blossoms brave bedeckèd daintily. "

Brave indeed, for not in the suburbs only but also in the city itself the Almond makes its joyful proclamation, "Lo, the winter is past, the rain is over and gone, the flowers appear on the earth, and the time of the singing of birds is come."

Andromeda floribunda, E.F.—Prefers peat, sand, and shade, and well deserves this special attention, being always green in leaf, shapely in form, and flowering with silver bells, resembling those of the Lily of the Valley, to "ring out the old, ring in the new."

Aralia (Japonica Sieboldii), *E.F.*—Has a sub-tropical appearance, and, when you first see it in a garden, looks as though it had escaped, like a canary from its cage, from the stove or greenhouse; but it is quite hardy here in Kent, and is very picturesque with its stately habit, its large lustrous leaves, and its ivy-like efflorescence.

Arbutus Unedo (the Tree Strawberry), *E.F.*—No one forgets this Arbutus who has seen it on the banks of Killarney Lakes. Nowhere else, no, not in the Riviera, is it so vivid in the colour of its leaf and fruit, but it is very beautiful in many of our English gardens, though we seldom see its scarlet berries; and if it is injured in our severer seasons, it has great recuperative power.

Artemisia (Southernwood), *E.*—Is somewhat limp and unattractive to the eye, but its fragrance makes a powerful appeal to the nose. Sixty years ago the farm lads wore it with a bit of gillyflower as a posy on their Sunday smocks.

Aucuba Japonica, *E.F.*—Like the friend that loveth at all times, and the brother born for adversity, is always charming and cheerful in a garden, with its bright vestments of green and gold, and most conspicuously in the winter's desolation and gloom. Even under trees it is *toujours gai*,[1] and in the smut and smoke of the town, with occasional ablutions, it still maintains its smile. It suggests a striking pictorial advertisement for the manufacturer of soap, who might contrast its appearance before and after the application of his suds.

There is a far more romantic association, such as might inspire another Darwin to write "The Loves of the Plants." For many lonely years the male Aucuba lived in celibacy, no female of his race dwelling in our land, but then a lady Aucuba in Japan had pity on his solitude, and came over the seas to be his bride. Sons they had and daughters fair, the latter displaying

---

[1] Like many of the Cyclamens, notably *C. Neapolitanum*.

in their brilliant scarlet berries the feminine love of adornment.

The Aucuba is improved in shape and brilliancy by a judicious application of the knife.

Azalea (Pontica, Ghent, and Mollis), *D.F.*—From North America, Europe, India, and China, unsurpassed in its glowing colours, as varied as they are vivid, from pure white and blushing rose to brilliant scarlet and gold. They are starved to death on the clay, and they are withered away from lack of moisture on the chalk, but in damp leaf-mould and in peat they are glorious.

The most gorgeous dazzling sight which eye could behold was once described to me by one who had seen it. On a lake in front of a country mansion there was a small island, covered with azalea and rhododendrons in full flower, and when he saw them in full sunshine the lady of the house went to the margin of the water and blew a silver whistle, whereupon a cloud of peacocks rose from the flowers and flew towards her, their bright plumage reflected in the lake !

Bambusa (Bamboo).—We have now such a profusion of ornamental grasses (the Kew Catalogue of *Gramineæ* gives a list of more than 130 varieties) that they should form a group in all extensive gardens, and I defer them accordingly for special consideration when we proceed to the arrangement of our beds, in the Great Garden.

Berberis, Mahonia (Barberry), *D.F.*—One of those distinguished inmates of the garden which a cricketer would designate as "good all round," charming alike in foliage, flower, and fruit—the latter enlivening the dulness of winter with its vermilion berries, like the scarlet coat of a huntsman in the hillside covert of gorse.

There are many pretty varieties, but I like *Aquifolium*, *Darwinii*, and *Thunbergii* most.

Bocconia cordata (from Japan), *D.F*—A pleasing shrub of free growth in good soil, having large leaves and flowers in feathery tufts, not of individual merit, but effective *en masse*.

I dare not commend the *Buddleia* as hardy, and therefore transfer my praise to

Buxus sempervirens (the common *Box*), *E.*, so familiar to us, as an edging to our walks, and to the slugs, as a screen from the heat and a shelter from the cold. Permitted to grow, it is a constant and charming shrub, and the Japanese variety with golden leaves should be in every garden. The Romans rejoiced to clip their *Buxus* into hideous representations of birds and beasts, and there have been heathens since in all times and climes, who have found pleasure in the same atrocious mutilations. The Christian keeps his trees and his animals distinct; he prefers the living peacock with his plumage spread, to his effigy done in yew : and when he cuts his evergreens, except to prune, it is to bring the fir-tree, and the pine-tree, and the box-tree together to beautify the place of the Sanctuary in the happy Christmastide.

Cercis (Judas Tree) *D.F.*, associated by tradition, from its sanguine tints, with the death-tree of the traitor, is an ornamental and striking object among our shrubs, though it has not in this country the vigour or the depth of colour which it displays in the Riviera. I shall never forget a tree of it which I saw in a villa near Nice, having its carmine-purple flowers intermixed with those of the golden Banksia rose, and the deep blue sky over all.

Would that I might include in my list the charming *Choisya ternata*, but it is not hardy enough for the open bed, although in sunny sites with shelter it delights us with the three leaflets which explain its title, *ternata*, and with the abundance of white flowers, which have suggested the more poetic designation of the Mexican Orange Blossom.

Cistus (Gum Cistus, Rock Rose), *E.F.*—There are certain flowers which, having once seen, we love for ever. Outside the garden, those which we gathered in childhood, the primrose, the violet, the cowslip, and the hedgerow rose, bring us, whenever we meet them, a momentary gleam of that brightness which the years make dim; and inside the garden few flowers have so much power to revive the past as the pretty rock rose with its circular white flowers, and its centre of indescribable colours, red and brown. The individual flowers are only for a few hours in bloom,

"A rose's brief, bright life of joy,"

but the tree produces a long succession of its ephemeral beauty. I have found the old variety quite hardy, and it was common once in the cottage gardens of the shires, although now it is rarely seen.

Cornus (Dogwood), *E.F.*—A valuable adjunct to our shrubberies for its free growth and manifold varieties of colour. The berries of *C. Mascula*, the Cornelian cherry, are beautiful, and the red stems, the gold and silver foliage, the white and yellow flowers, are admirable in themselves, and contrast with more sombre companions. *C. aurea elegantissima*, *Variegata*, and *Benthamia fragrans* should be grown. They thrive best in peat.

Cratægus (the Thorn), *D.F.*—There are few objects in our English landscapes of such distinctive beauty as the great hawthorn hedges which surround our pastures and meads, when the air is "sweet scented with the May," and when there is a verdure around us which no other land can show. Charming also are the thorns in our parks. I like them best in clumps, intermixed, white, pink, and red, in our hedges and shrubberies; and, sparsely introduced, in the large mixed beds which I advocate for our gardens, and for which I am in this list selecting the component parts. *Paul's Scarlet* takes precedence of all.

I have already referred to *C. Pyracantha* as one of the most desirable of our mural climbers. It is best on a wall, but it may be tastefully arranged in beds.

Cydonia (The Quince), *D.F.*, again reminds us of a beloved old friend, *Pyrus Japonica* (Japanese Quince), whom we have already greeted with an enthusiastic welcome, when, leaning against the walls of our home, we saw his ruddy features through our window-pane; but we must not forget to cultivate elsewhere the other varieties of Cydonia, white, pink, crimson, and scarlet, which make such a pleasant diversity in our borders and beds, They may sometimes require the pruning-knife to check irregularity of growth, and to induce conformity with their surroundings.

Cytisus (Broom), *D.F.*—The golden and white Broom, *Andreanus* and *Albus*, must be included in our *tableaux vivans*; but the pride and glory of the *Cytisus* family, the pride and glory of many a cottage home, and beautiful exceedingly wherever it grows, is that fountain of gold, the *Laburnum*.

Daphne (Mezereon), *D.E.F.*, is another of those flowers which, when it brings to us in February the sweet perfume of its purple flowers, recalls to us those places which still seem to us the fairest on earth, and to some of us those faces "which we have loved long since, and lost awhile." *Mezereon flore albo* should have a place in our gardens, but neither should occupy a conspicuous position, as they are uninteresting when not in flower. *D. laureola*, the Spurge Laurel, and *D. pontica* are pretty evergreen shrubs ; and *D. Cneorum*, the least of the family, growing close to the ground, has the daintiest flowers, of a lively pink, and the most delicious, spicy, and refreshing scent.

I must pass *Desfontainia spinosa* with a sigh, even as a coinless schoolboy goes by a confectioner's shop, because there are few gardens so highly favoured as to produce its scarlet and orange flowers. I have heard, but I have not seen, that it thrives on a wall.

Deutzia, D.F, requires no such warming apparatus. It is quite hardy, and its pretty leafage and clusters of white flowers, with a roseate tinge, well deserve the eulogy of its descriptive titles, *candidissima flore pleno* and *gracilis*.

Can any one tell me why the Deutzia is called " The Pride of Rochester." The Deutzias come from China, Japan, and Mexico, but this gives no clue. There is a fair and famous city called Rochester in the State of New York, but my friend, Mr. George Ellwanger, who lives there, and has not only given us that charming book, "The Garden Story," but is, so far as I know the most distinguished horticulturist in America, recognises the title, but makes no claim. At the Rochester in England, where I have the high honour to be Dean, I can find no record of its origin. I have heard our vocalists express a desire, " I'd like to be a flower," but I never heard them sing or say that they wish to be a Deutzia.

Although I have seen the *Escallonia macrantha* flourishing profusely, forming boundaries high and wide, with

I

its glossy foliage and dark red flowers in the garden of
my friend, the Rector of Kilkhampton, North Cornwall, I cannot regard it as hardy, except on walls whereon
it grows luxuriantly ; but the

Euonymus (Spindle Tree), *E.D.F.*, will not disappoint us,
presenting itself in great variety, from the tree, *Lati-
folius*, to the lovely *Radicans* with its silver leaves, alike
attractive on our rockeries, as a most effective edging
for our beds, or as a climber on our walls. *Flavescens,
Japonicus,* and *Aureo-marginatus* deserve annexation.

Forsythia suspensa and *vindissima, D.F.,* with "the airy grace
of their golden sprays," must be grown in all gardens.
Suspensa should be suspended, that is, planted on a
bank, having its drooping branches covered with flowers.

Genista Anglica (the English Gorse), which is sometimes
classified under *Ulex Europæus*, but belongs to the
former allocation. Canon Ellacombe, in his delightful
book on "The Plant-Lore of Shakespeare," informs us
that the "pricking goss," of which Ariel speaks in the
fourth act of "The Tempest," was the *Genista Anglica,*
or petty Whin. We do not introduce it into our gardens, restricting ourselves to the Spanish and German
varieties, because we see it outside on our commons
and coverts in such abundant glory. I have met with
it, nevertheless, cherished in a pot and protected by a
frame, in a garden near Albany, U.S.A., where the
accomplished lady of the house had "a Shakespearian
collection." Linnæus, it is said, knelt and wept, overcome with admiration, when he first looked upon a
vast expanse of its golden bloom ; but there is another
incident which, with the most sincere respect for
Linnæus, I cannot refrain from repeating, and which
reveals to us a very different strain of emotions associated with gorse. I heard it told by an eye-witness,

in a pathetic tone, of a huntsman who had drawn a
large gorse covert, always reserved for special occasions,
for the first time blank. "I can assure you," said the
historian, "that when the hounds came out, I saw a tear
fall from his face." "In my opinion," spake a callous
critic, "the morning must have been bitterly cold, and
it was not a tear."

Hibiscus Syriacus (Syrian Mallow), *Althæa frutex*, and "Rose
of Sharon." *D.F.* I shall never forget my happy surprise, when examining, many years ago, in the early
autumn, a large border of crowded shrubs in my garden,
I came suddenly upon a compact bush in full leaf and
flower of *Althæa frutex.* I had never seen it before in
bloom, and as "all its lovely companions," the flowering shrubs, "were faded and gone," it was indeed a
thing of beauty and a joy for ever. I noted its family
likeness to the *Hibiscus* in my stove, but the resemblance
only increased my astonishment. One does not expect
to see the lords and ladies of the salon standing like

> "Nicodamus and the goddess Vanus,"

uncovered in the open air.

Mine was the common variety with purple flowers,
but there are now many others, white, pink, violet,
crimson, with single and double flowers. They must
have good soil.

Hydrangea, D.F.—This bright floriferous shrub does not
receive the favours which it deserves from the gardener.
It is easily propagated from cuttings, recovers from
prostration by frost, and needs no special cultivation,
although it shows a preference for certain climatic surroundings and ferruginous soils. In parts of Ireland,
for example, it attains remarkable size and beauty ; but
the most charming specimens which I have seen grow

in the gardens of Penrhyn Castle in North Wales, and are richly tinted with a deep and vivid blue. *Hydrangea paniculata superba* is the belle of the family, and everywhere, even in the Royal Gardens at Kew, where it has so many rivals, it wins, with its large clusters of snowy flowers, the admiration of all. It requires close pruning in spring and liberal diet.

Ilex (Holly).—First and foremost our English holly (*Aqui-folium*), always beautiful, from the little seedling to the tall pyramidal tree. We lose much enjoyment by the restriction of our attachments to full-grown plants and trees. I know a certain class of so-called gardeners who have never a word of praise for many rare and excellent specimens, because they have seen them "much larger," just as some of our modern gunners appraise the quality of their sport by the quantity of fat pheasants laid out in line.

What a possession is a long old holly screen! impervious to the eyes of the curious, the entrance of the schoolboy or the tramp, everywhere presenting among its scarlet berries the sharp points of its prickly leaves, like the bayonets of a regiment glistening in the sun.

And then "its infinite variety"—in stature, tall and short ; in foliage (always so bright, so constant, and so clean), large and broad (*latifolia*), small and narrow (*angustifolia*), golden (*foliis aureis*), silver (*foliis argenteis*), here almost spineless, and there so covered with its piercing thorns, thick as the quills upon the fretful porcupine, that it is called the Hedgehog ; and with berries white, yellow, and red.

The cheeriest of all our Christmas decorations, the chief adornment of the great bush in the servants' hall, among the oranges and the apples, the gay ribbons and

paper flowers, when all the members met around it and
the village choir sang lustily—

> "God bless the master of this house,
> The misteress also,
> Likewise the little childeren,
> That round the table go."

And when "the family retired," there were "cakes and
ale" (the superiority of water as a winter beverage was
not as yet revealed), "and for awhile it was merry in
the hall"; and I venture to believe that although we
had no railways in the days of which I write (seventy
years ago) [1] no telephones, no photographs, "living" or
otherwise, we were as sincere in our Christianity, as
happy in our homes, and as kind one towards another,
as our illuminated descendants in this year, 1899.

Indigofera Gerardiana, D.F., with an exposure to the south,
a slight screen from the north, and a little mulching
in winter (a large number of our outdoor plants, though
they do not require, are all the better for an overcoat),
is an elegant shrub, with pretty drooping foliage, and
dainty little rosy-purple flowers.   From *I. tinctoria*, extensively grown in India, we get the beautiful blue dye.

Juniperus (Juniper), *F.*—An ancient, constant, and munificent
benefactor to the guild of gardeners—erect (*Hibernica*),
and drooping (*pendula*), pyramidal (*excelsa*), and growing
close to the ground, like the beautiful Savin (*tamariscifolia*) ; of varied tints, all shades of green, and glaucous
(*glauca*), but honoured the most in its golden garments
(*chinensis aurea*), wherewith it enlivens always, but chiefly
when

> "The day is dull, and dark, and dreary,
> It rains, and the wind is never weary,"

---

[1] The Liverpool and Manchester Railway was opened Sept. 15,
1833.

around our cloud-capped towers. The juniper has other merits, besides that of gladdening the sight. The wood is hard and fragrant, the oil is precious, the berries are medicinal ; and all these good qualities must be accepted as solace by those who deplore the facts, that Gin is an abbreviation of Geneva, and that Geneva does not refer to the city of that name, but to the old French *genevre,* which means *juniper;* and that the berries of the plant have been long and largely used in the concoction of a liquor which has probably done more to promote the worst forms of intoxication than all other alcoholic drinks in conjunction.

Kalmia, latifolia, E.F.—Unsurpassed, like the old Gallica rose, *Rien ne me surpasse,* when grown in its perfection, with its profusion of waxlike, roseate flowers ; but this can only be done in places where peat is found in abundance, and not brought in a barrow. You may import splendid specimens, "set with bloom," and enjoy a brief efflorescence, but your plants will gradually deteriorate. At Bagshot, the Kalmia is a bewilderment of beauty, and we that dwell on chalk or on clay, sigh dolefully as we gaze, and say, Oh that these flowers were as hardy as those which grow on the

Kerrya, which came from Japan (*Japonica*), strikes freely under a hand-glass, grows vigorously, and flowers abundantly, plant it where you will.

Alas, for the debility of human affection ! if the wish were granted, would not the love in many hearts—not in yours or mine, but in the case of inferior persons—be endangered by familiarity, and become first tepid and then cold ? It is a perilous temptation, even to those who love flowers the best, not only to exaggerate, as we have shown, the importance of size, but also to depreciate the worth of common things. When we find

ourselves among lords and ladies, we cannot be expected
to retain all our former veneration for baronets and
squires. The sense of apotheosis is felt by us all, which
glowed in the breast of the promoted ploughman when
he sang—

> " And little Nell I loved so well,
>   And walked so wi' o' Sundays—
> ' Good Lor,' says I, ' don't talk to me,
>   I'se mon at Mestur Grundy's ! ' "

"How can you grow that rubbishy *Kerrya ?*" I was
asked; "every pig-jobber has it in his garden." "And
why," I replied, "do you desire to concentrate all the
interest and energy of the pig-jobber on swine and
sausage and swill ? Why may not he admire as much
as I do the bright yellow flowers of the Kerrya, single
or double ? On your principle I must expel from my
garden some of its fairest inmates—lilacs, cloves—must
turn traitor, and seek to dethrone the flower which is
queen of all. According to your views I must eliminate
the

Laburnum, D.F., so familiar and dear to us all, that I need
only say that the Scotch laburnum (*Albinum*) prolongs
our enjoyment, being somewhat later in bloom ; that
Pendulum, on a standard, makes a *fons splendidior vitro ;*
and that Waterer and Parks have introduced two new
varieties which seem to be improvements both in size
and colour." The laburnum is better known than
grown, rarely receiving that which it often requires,
the visit of an artist with a pruning-knife in his hand.
Thus trained, "it affords," as Philip Miller writes, "a
very agreeable prospect."

Lathyrus (the Everlasting Pea), D.F., must be among the
treasures which we are selecting for distribution in our
garden beds, although, belonging to the nomadic tribes,

it is addicted to trespass and requires perpetual restraint. Like a naughty child, it is always getting out
of its bed ; and it resembles also a certain spinster, a
most indefatigable district visitor, who was perpetually
tapping, like a woodpecker, at the study door of her
rector, until he confided to a friend, who betrayed his
confidence, that "dear Mary Jane was one of those
persons, whom you could neither do with nor without."

The vagaries of the *Lathyrus* will yield to treatment,
and if it is now and then too demonstrative in its atten-
tions to a neighbour, or encroaches on the sward, like
a reckless undergraduate in the College "Quad"—

" If to the plant some venial errors fall,
Look at the flowers and you'll forget them all."

Laurus (Laurel), *E.*—We will not linger among the laurels,
although they were one of childhood's favourite haunts,
when we went forth to hide or to seek, to spy or to be
spied ; although we learned at school to revere the
laurel as the tree of Apollo, which, by a special order
from Jupiter Tonaus, no lightning was allowed to touch,
and which crowned the great heroes and poets of their
day ; because useful in the shrubberies, it is too dull
and monotonous for our present purpose, and must
make way for the *Viburnum* (which we call *Laurus*)
Tinus, and of which we shall have to speak.

Ligustrum (Privet), *E.*—In the month of November 1898,
and in the Royal Gardens of Kew, I saw a row of
Golden Privet, bright as a beacon fire, and my hand
went instinctively to my notebook, as though I had
been a reporter, and Lord Salisbury rose to speak. I
have lost my memorandum, but the variety, I feel sure,
was *aureum elegantissimum.*

Magnolia, E.D.F.—The brave gardener, whose happy lot

is fallen in those parts of our land where the climate
is the least severe, will not be satisfied with *M. grandiflora* on his walls (see page 100), but will make experiment in sheltered places of *Conspicua, Hypoleuca,
Kobus, Obovata, Purpurea,* and *Watsoni.* One success
will console for half-a-dozen disappointments.

Mespilus (the Medlar), should be planted in the shrubbery,
not in the orchard, being far more admirable for its
vernal flowers and its autumnal foliage than for the
fruit, which is insipid and suggestive of decay.

The *Snowy Mespilus* belongs to another denomina-
tion, *Amelanchier,* and with its pretty white flowers,
pendulous like the snowdrop, and its leaves so finely
cut that it has the second appellation of the *Fringe Tree,*
must be received with all honour into " Our Selection."

Olearia Haasti, E.F.—Here in Kent a charming and compact
evergreen shrub, delighting us in the summer with a
long continuance of its white fragrant flowers in panicles.

Pernettya, E.F.—There are certain plants and flowers, which
from time to time surprise us with their beauty, arrest
and absorb us, as when we come suddenly on a glorious
landscape, a sunset, or a lovely little child. Wherefore
I was not surprised to hear the exclamation, "Oh, what
a sweet!" from a lady who beheld for the first time
this pretty shrub covered with its fruit. The flowers
are white, the berries are red, and the best varieties are
angustifolia, mucronata, and *speciosa.* It likes peat.

The Phillyrea, E., should be in our collection of evergreens,
although its flowers are meagre, for the sake of its dark
green foliage. *Vilmoriana* is the best variety.

Prunus Pisardi, D.F.—I am troubled to find that my supply
of complimentary adjectives is exhausted and weak. I
have gone through the alphabet *da capo,* and now such
words as admirable, beautiful, charming, delicious, ex-

quisite, fascinating, gorgeous, handsome, inimitable, jubi-
lant, kingly, lovely, magnificent, noble, overpowering,
queenly, rare, splendid, transcendent, unique, wonderful,
seem to have lost their power.   I derive no help from
the laudatory epithets which are now in fashion.   I
cannot say of a sweet pea that it is "ripping," or of a lily
that it is "stunning," or of an orchid that it is "awfully
jolly."

What shall I say, then, in my present dearth of diction,
in praise of one of my greatest favourites, *Prunus Pisardi?*
I gratefully avail myself of a description I find elsewhere :[1]   "This is the best hardy tree that has been
introduced in late years.   The foliage and bark are of a
dark purple, surpassing the Purple Beech in richness of
colour, the leaves also remaining on the tree much
longer.   In spring there are clusters of very pretty
flowers, which produce nice fruit in autumn."   With
the exception of "the nice fruit in autumn," which I
have not yet seen in my garden, either in Kent or
Nottinghamshire, I heartily endorse this eulogy.   It is
most to be admired in the sunshine of the early
spring, and it is not only beautiful in itself but it
enhances the beauty of its neighbours, as the brunette
the blonde.

We must also have the *Double-blossomed Plum*
(*Domestica*), and the *Double-blossomed Sloe* (*Spinosa*),
the white and pink varieties of *Sinensis Japonica*
and *Triloba.*

Pyrus (the Pear), *D.E.*, recalls to us elderly folk our early
admirations of those favourite trees which have had our
lifelong love.   *P. Sorbus aria*, the indigenous *White
Beam Tree*, so conspicuous in our plantations from the

---

[1] Catalogue of Messrs. R. Smith & Co., Nurseries, Worcester.

silver lining of its leaves ; *P. aucuparia*, the *Mountain Ash*, not quite so vivid and brilliant on this side the Border as the Rowan of the Highlands ; and *P. Malus Prunifolia* (what a conglomeration of pear, apple, and plum !) the *Siberian Crab*, which, when all our pockets bulged with green fruit, hard and sour, we ate without preparation, but now prefer as jam.

There are other beautiful Crabs : the Transparent Crab, *Malus Astracanica*, the Dartmouth, and the John Downie ; but the most fascinating of all is *P. Malus Floribunda*, of which Mr. Robinson writes in the "English Flower Garden," "Fully grown, with a dense wide-spreading head of slender branches, loaded every May with a profusion of flowers, of pale pink when expanded, and of a brilliant crimson in the bud, they are most beautiful. *No garden is well planted, if this tree is wanting,* as it is hardy, grows rapidly anywhere, and costs little to buy."

The fruit delights, as a curiosity—an apple, perfect in form, about the size of a pill !   Gulliver must have seen them in the fruiterers' stalls in Liliput, and I have seen them in the same proportion to the persons who were supposed to enjoy them, on a toy dish at a doll's dessert. There are two other desirable varieties of *P. M. floribunda, atrosanguinea* and *Scheideckeri.*

Retinospora, E., is described by Sir Joseph Paxton (Botanical Dictionary) as a genius of conifers, not unlike *Cupressus,* and is a very precious importation from Japan.   Especially the golden varieties of *Filifera, Obtusa, Pisifera,* and *Plumosa,* and the silver variety, *Albo-picta.*   The Retinosporas like shelter, but not so near as to exclude the sun.

Rhododendrons, E.F., should be largely grown, wherever they flourish abundantly, as at Bagshot, or in Cornwall, or at Cobham Hall in Kent, where they surround the fish-pond, admiring themselves in its waters, but not where their bones, that is their stems, protrude through their foliage, that is their flesh ; and there should be a liberal selection of the fittest and not of the few, as in so many instances, where the superannuated *Ponticum* still reigns supreme, or where you might infer that there were only two or three varieties, whereas there are two or three hundred. I do not propose to plant rhododendrons in the beds, for which we are now selecting materials, because they will not grow in ordinary soil, and where happily they will grow elsewhere, must be placed with American and other companions, who rejoice in peat.

It must indeed be confessed that some of our floral favourites are fastidious in their diet, like some of our social friends, who shriek, "No sugar !" as if they were going to be poisoned, "One lump !" "Two lumps !" "No cream !" but the true gardener, like the true lover, rejoices to discover and gratify the inclinations of his beloved, and so wins a sweet success. The process is sometimes disheartening ; in both cases there may be a coyness, an unwillingness to expand, an indication of blight, which, though it will ultimately yield to treatment, for a while will perplex and pain ; and he therefore enjoys all the more those happier seasons in which his patience is no longer tried, when there are no whims to worry, no defeats to fear, but the object of his affections greets him with a smile, and receives with a benignant sympathy the attention which he rejoices to bestow. The meaning of my allegory is, that while there are plants comparatively few, which require special soil and study, the great majority are easily cultivated in all good gardens, and that one of the best of them is

Rhus (the Sumach), *D.F.*, the parent of a most healthful, handsome family, of whom it might be said,—

> " Sons he had and daughters fair,
> And days of strength and glory."

They are all remarkable for their good looks, *Glabra Laciniata, Typhina,* " the Stag's Horn," *Osbeckii, Vernicifera,* and in form and colour most ornamental, reminding us in their autumnal vestments, scarlet and golden, of the glory of an American " Fall " ; but the most wonderful of them all is the *Venetian Sumach, Cotinus.* It is indescribable, and the scientific definition of its efflorescence, *loose panicles of elongated hairy pedicels,* does not enlighten the ordinary mind. There is a similitude of smoke amid its rosy-purple flowers, which gives the idea of fire, and has suggested the name of " the Burning Bush."

Requiring ample room, and being attractive for the greater part of the year, the Sumachs should have a bed to themselves.

As a sweet little maid, aged seven, sometimes rushes into my study to announce with joyous excitement, " Grandpa, the soldiers are coming ! " and I hear the music of their band, so the pretty pink blossoms of the Flowering Currant,

Ribes Sanguinea, D.F., are among the foremost and fairest daughters of the year, who come to tell us of the advent of spring, and with the spring,

Rosa, D.F., the Queen of the Garden !—The Dean must have a special Chapter on the Rose.

Sambucus (the Elder) *D.F.*—*Racemosa,* with its scarlet berries, and *Phimosa,* with its fern-like leaves, are desirable for the shrubberies ; and *Aurea* is very striking so long as it retains its golden hues ; but this period is of uncertain duration, and too often and too soon is followed by an appearance of "green and yellow melancholy," and by a reversion to type. We must hope for more satisfactory results from *Sambucus Racemosa foliis aureis*, which is said to be a great improvement, and has received an Award of Merit from the Royal Horticultural Society. The silver-leaved *Argenteo Variegata* is pronounced by Mr. Ellwanger, of Rochester, New York, and there is no more reliable authority, as being "one of the best variegated shrubs," and it also thrives in a town garden.

Spiræa (Meadow-sweet), *D.F.*—We often hear of an *embarras des richesses*, but I cannot remember a case, nor have I witnessed among my fellow-men a reluctance to encounter the risk. When Mr. Andrew Carnegie, "the Iron King," wrote his interesting treatise on "The Gospel of Wealth," he severely censured those who spent their lives in heaping up riches for themselves and their heirs, and declared it to be a disgrace to die with great accumulations of wealth. I was told at Pittsburgh, the city of the King, that a working man had written to the author his admiration of the principles which he had so powerfully enforced, and at the same time his painful anxiety, lest by some sudden calamity the degradation which he had denounced should happen to the evangelist himself. He, the working man, was prepared accordingly to diminish the danger by a prompt acceptance of one million dollars, and if this relief was inadequate, he had friends on whom he could rely to make a further reduction ; but there was no *embarras*. And so when we come to the *Spiræas*, and find on the lists of the Royal Gardens at Kew one hundred and fifty varieties (shrubby and herbaceous), in our nurseries and private gardens so many attractive specimens, in our books and catalogues such glowing descriptions of a plant which is as hardy as it is beautiful ; of its easy culture, distinct habit, fine form, and gracefully drooping plumes ; of its flowers, creamy white, tipped with red, pink, rosy crimson, carmine, we proceed without embarrassment to make our selection.   Even as a schoolboy, *magna componere parvis*, who has received a golden " tip " from his uncle, wastes no time in a tedious scrutiny of the confectioner's stores, but devotes himself at once to those dainties which are dear to his experience, or have been highly commended by his mates, so let us at once select from the *Spiræas* those which from our own culture we know to be excellent, and those which have the approbation of experts in whom we surely confide.   Ocular inspection and the consensus of these experts, which may be ascertained from the lists of the nurserymen, and from the reports of the Floral Committee of the Royal Horticultural Society, are the best guides for the amateur gardener of the herbaceous *Spiræas*, which are few in comparison with the shrubby.   The best are *Aruncus*, " the Goat's Beard " (whoever named this variety paid a preposterous compliment to the goat) ; *Lobata*, which has a far more appropriate designation as " Queen of the Prairies " ; and *Palmata*.   Of the shrubby or bush *Spiræas*, the most eligible are *Ariæfolia, Bella, Bumalda,* "Anthony Waterer," *Callosa, Confusa, Douglasii, Grandiflora, Lævigata, Lindleyana, Opulifolia, Prunifolia, Thunbergii, Ulmifolia.*   It is sad to reject so many candidates, but "the fact is," as Mr. Robinson writes,[1] " we have now too great a number of *Spiræas*, and too great a similarity among them, flowering at the same time.   No collection need number more than a dozen kinds to represent the finest

---

[1] "English Flower Garden," p. 775.

types of beauty in flower and growth ; and these would produce much better effect in a group, than when dotted among other shrubs of diverse habits, and never displaying the free growth which is one of their greatest charms. My dozen would include the following kinds, which are placed according to their average heights, beginning with the tallest, *Lindleyana, Ariœfolia, Douglasii, Trilobata var Van Houttei, Prunifolia fl. pl., Japonica superba, Confusa, Canescens var flagellata, Contoniensis, Bella, Thunbergi, Japonica Thunbergi*, and *Japonica Bumalda*.

We shall do well to remember these words, and to obey this edict of the King of Spades, when we proceed to make arrangements in our Great Garden : meanwhile, I am perplexed as to the meaning of *Canescens flagellata*— who is the female "growing grey and whipped ? " We do not whip the worst of our women ; we are, on the contrary, too abstemious in flagellating the worst of our men. Does it refer to the treatment of some aged hound of the feminine gender, deaf or disobedient, at the hands of the second whip ? And if this be so, what resemblance is there between the dog, " the cat," and the *Spirœa ?*

The *Staphylea*, D.F., claims a place for its beautiful clusters of pure white and fragrant flowers.

The *Stuartias*, D.F., have a brilliant reputation. I have not seen them in our gardens, but my friend Dr. Marsters tells me that he remembers *S. Virginica* flowering in his father's garden forty years ago. Mr. Peter Henderson, the head of the famous firm at New York, writing of them in the country from which come *S. Virginica* and *J. pentagyna*, two of the three species most commonly known, describes them as " a genus of very beautiful, hardy, deciduous shrubs, allied to the Camellia, forming bushes

of handsome shape, growing from six to ten feet in
height, with flowers like a single rose about three inches
across, the petals of which are of a soft creamy white,
surrounding a tuft of deep crimson stamens, a charming
contrast to the pale green foliage. *S. pseudo-camellia*,
the third variety in cultivation, resembles the other two
in growth, foliage, and habit, but the flowers are larger
and whiter, and have yellow stamens.

Mr. Veitch speaks of *S. pseudo-camellia* as one of the
best flowering shrubs which we have received from
Japan, on account of its lovely flowers and the brilliant
autumnal tints of its foliage, crimson and gold. On the
same high authority (and what authority can be higher
than his, who imports the plant, grows it at home, and
reports progress ?) we are assured that

Styrax Obassia, *D.F.*, is one of the finest, if not the finest of
the small profuse flowering trees in which the Flora
of Japan is so rich.   It has an imposing foliage of bright
lustrous green, and the flowers are produced in great profusion, as in the well-known *Styrax Japonica*.   In Japan
they grow into tall trees from twenty to thirty feet in
height, and if when acclimatised they attain this altitude
with us, they will be among the finest of our lawn trees.

In gardens where the Camellia will flower out of
doors, as on the slopes of Belvoir, or in those glens
of Cornwall which descend to the banks of the Fal,
the *Stuartia* and the *Storax* should be grown, not in the
bleak places and the poor soils of the land.   Even in
the most favoured spots the planter must wait and hope
until his plants are established.   In this, as in many
other instances, the gardener like the husbandman must
have long patience.

Syringa (the Lilac), *D.F.*—I have read that traces of this
shrub have been found, in a stunted and sickly condi-

K

tion, among the ruins of some of our old castles, which have not been inhabited for 300 years. Other writers affirm that it came from Persia at a later period, although the variety which we call *Persica* was of subsequent introduction to the common blue Lilac, *S. vulgaris.* Many additions have been made to this family from China and Japan, *e.g. Oblata,* which was brought from a garden at *Shanghai* by Mr. Robert Fortune; and we have them in many colours, with single and double flowers. White—*Marie Legraye* (the best), *Japonica Alba grandiflora, Madame Lemoine.* Purple — *Josikœa, Latour D'Auvergne, Scipion Cochet.* Reddish lilac—*Souvenir de Spath,* and *Charles the X.*

There are many others, differing in form and colour, and it may be of superior merit in the estimation of the floral critic, but the old favourite is the most beloved of all. "During the time these shrubs are in flower there are very few others comparable to them for beauty or sweetness,"[1] and they bring us every year pathetic associations, sad memories, and brighter hopes.

Linnæus changed the title of this Genus from Lilac to *Syringa*, from the Greek συριγξ and the Latin *syringa, the Pipe-tree*, because it was the custom of those nations to extract the pith from the larger branches, and to make from the latter pipes for music ; and at the same time he gave the name of *Philadelphus* to the shrub which was and is commonly called *Syringa*, and is also known as *the mock Orange.*

S. Grandiflora, in good soil and with ample space, is one of the most magnificent of all flowering shrubs, covered with its white blossom, and fragrant even to "aromatic pain," and the miniature *P. microphyllus,*

---

[1] Philip Miller.

which has a much more agreeable odour, and Lemoine's hybrid, a cross between *microphylla* and *coronaria*, and of intermediate size, will add greatly to the manifold delights of a garden.

In the leafless, songless, sunless days of our wintry months, how one longs for the Lilac ; and how surely and sweetly it comes to brighten our gloom, by the cottage homes of the poor, and, with all the perfection of its flowers and its fragrance, in the Archbishop's garden at Lambeth.

Taxus (the Yew), *F.*—Why Taxus ? Proud of my county, "Olde Nottinghame," which bore upon its banner at Agincourt "an archere, clade in greene," and being myself a toxophilite, I prefer Pliny's derivation, from τοξος, a bow, and I dislike the suggestion of τοξικον, a poison, as reminding me of the death of a favourite cow, from eating the leaves of yew branches, thrown out of a plantation ; and also of an incident which exposed me for a time to the jeer and ridicule of my friends. One morning I was summoned from my breakfast to see an elderly female, a pattern of neatness, cleanliness, and modest behaviour, who showed me a petition, signed by several respectable neighbours, and asking help to replace her only cow, which had died from eating the leaves of a Yew. Her widow's cap, her silvery hair, her becoming deference, the sympathies of our common bereavement, worked upon my feelings to the extent of half-a-sovereign. Two days after a policeman came to inform me that a gang of impostors were going about obtaining money on the pretence of having lost cows from poison, and he hoped that I would at once inform him if any of them came to me. I complied with his request, and, strange to say, I fulfilled my promise. From some lack of organisation (perhaps the sweet old lady disappeared with the ten shillings without reporting progress), another scamp (of the masculine gender) paid me a visit, was delivered to the officer, and consigned by the magistrate to six weeks' involuntary gymnastics, on the tread-mill of the jail.

The Yew has strong claims upon the grateful admiration of the gardener. In a few years *T. baccata* forms as a hedge an effectual protection, where the stormy winds do blow ; and *T. aurea variegata*, with its golden leaves, is always one of the brightest ornaments of his garden. *T. fastigiata*, the Irish Yew, is too sombre in colour and severe in form for much repetition, but where it is sparsely and tastefully planted it is an agreeable adjunct to the scene. The larger golden yews should be planted *en masse* or as a central group, with appropriate surroundings. They make a charming hedge.

Viburnum (the Guelder Rose), *D.F.*, producing the pretty white globular flowers, with which we children renewed the " snowball" contests of the winter, until both armies suddenly fled from their *bataille des fleurs*, at the approach of the head gardener. Why this *Viburnum* should be described as *sterilis*, when it is so much more suggestive of the old lady in the shoe, is a problem which I cannot solve.

There is another of this family, the *Viburnum* or *Laurus tinus*, beloved by all who love a garden, trying to console us with its green leaves, red buds, and white flowers when we most need consolation ; trying to make us believe that it is summer, when the winds howl, and the rains drench, like Mark Tapley, blithe and jolly, and shouting "Hurra for Eden!" in the midst of sickness and all the other miseries which flesh is heir to.

Weigela de la premiere qualité, D.F., among flowering shrubs, symmetrical, bright, bountiful, flowers varying in colour from white (*candida* and *hortensis*), pale rose (*amabilis*), to crimson red (*Eva Rathke, Lavalléi,* and *Voltaire Looymansii*), must be included in the selection.

The *Weigelas* are quite hardy, but he who would see them in their most perfect phase must give them a wall with a south aspect.

Between these shrubs, evergreen and deciduous, and the turf surrounding, we must arrange plants of a lower and diminutive growth, which shall completely cover the ground. There is no more necessity for large spaces of brown earth in the beds than for the exhibition of bare patches of canvas here and there in a picture. Flat stones may be introduced here and there among these plants, which are commonly known as "Alpine," but we do not wish to inspect the soil. Here is

A LIST OF PLANTS SUITABLE FOR THE EDGING OF BEDS

(WITH POWER TO ADD TO THEIR NUMBER)

Acæna.	Arenaria Balearica.
Ajuga.	Aubrietia.
Alyssum.	Bambusa pigmæa.
Arabis.	Buxus Japonica aurea.

Campanula alpina.
Candy tuft.
China Roses.
Cotoneaster Simonsii.
Dianthus alpinus.
Daphne Cneorum.
Epigæa Repens.
Ericas in variety.
Euonymus radicans varie-
    gata.
Festucas.
Gaultheria procumbens.
Gentiana acaulis.
Helianthemum.
Hedera.
Helleborus.
Hypericum.
Juniper tamariscifolia.
Lithospermum.

Myosotis.
Narcissus dwarf.
Potentilla dwarf.
Phlox.
Ruscus.
Santolina.
Saxifrage.
Sedum.
Sempervivum.
Skimmia Japonica.
Spiræa dwarf.
Thalictrum minus.
Thyme.
Tiarella Cordifolia.
Trifolium alpinum.
Triteleia uniflora.
Veronica repens.
Vinca.

With the frequent addition of pillar roses, clematis, and other climbers on poles (Canon Ellacombe, in " A Gloucestershire Garden," commends
Smilax and *Asparagus Vertici* and *Medeoloides* as
hardy and of extreme beauty), there will be found
in the lists preceding an abundance of material for
the composite beds in the chief garden. These
beds must be of sufficient dimensions to contain
such evergreen and deciduous shrubs, and flowers,
as will make them interesting and pleasant to the
eye throughout the seasons of the year. With

their broad separations of grass they will occupy
a great extent of ground, and the main design
of my ideal garden is, as I have said, for long
purses and large ambitions, but it may be
modified and adapted; the beds may be many
or few.

Of course there will be failures. "I educate
myself on my mistakes," writes our Laureate in
"*The Garden that I Love.*" "Every error should
be a stepping-stone to something better," writes
"*Elizabeth in her German Garden.*" As to
growth, there will be success and defeat.
Contrasts by which we proposed to make our
neighbours green with envy will be regarded
with apathy. It may be, that some favourite
is missing, gone to the Crematorium; but the
gardener is not dismayed. He has his pruning-
knife, he can transplant, and rearrange.

Other beds of distinct genera might be added,
a group of Pampas grass, of Bamboos and
Eulalias, of Rhododendrons and American plants,
with lilies intermixed, where peat is available,
of Spiræas, and Yuccas.

These elaborate suggestions are only offered to
those who are about to lay out a new garden

regardless of expense, but I venture to add that
whatever may be the breadth of the ground, or
the length of the purse, the principles which I
advocate might in most instances be accepted
with a sure success, namely, that there should be

More grass and less gravel,
More flowers and less bare soil,
More curves and fewer straight lines and angles,
More hardy and not so many " half-hardy " plants,
More arrangement and less disorder,
More shrubs, evergreen and golden, to " cheer the
ungenial day."

We pass now from the beds to the outer
boundary of the great garden, and to

CHAPTER VII

The Herbaceous Border

"*In all places then, and in all seasons,*
Flowers expand their light and soul-like wings.
Teaching us by most persuasive reasons
How akin they are to human things.
And with child-like credulous affection
We behold their tender buds expand,
Emblems of our own great resurrection,
Emblems of the bright and better land."
—LONGFELLOW.

MANIFOLD and gracious have been the additions and improvements which have come in recent years, and which are continually coming to our gardens — cheap glass, importations from all parts of the world, a more intelligent culture, bequeathed by the great gardeners, who are gone, to their sons, who have had in addition a more competent education; but there has been no introduction which has had such happy and universal influence in extending and increasing the enjoyment of a garden as the Herbaceous Border.   It is for all; for the rich, though they have consigned it for the present to the kitchen garden, doubtful until they hear from the Duke's gardener as to a closer intercourse; and to the poor—why, there is hardly a prettier sight than the narrow little path from the highway to the cottage door through beds of bright and fragrant flowers!

The dimensions of the Herbaceous Border, which should consist of the best soil to be had, well drained, well dug, and well dunged, should be in length, the longer the better, in breadth ten to twelve feet.   Should the collection be miscellaneous or in groups? in numerous or in select varieties?   Should we be satisfied with the flowers in their sequence wherever they may appear in our beds, or should we omit those which bloom earlier in the year in order that we have a simultaneous and splendid display?   If we can afford a spring garden for our

Aconites, Snowdrops, Crocuses, Hyacinths, Narcissus, Scillas, first Iris, Tulips, and any other
efflorescence, "which comes before the swallow
dare"; or if the itinerant Dives has three or four
places which he visits at different seasons of the
year; it may be well in such cases to fill the
Herbaceous Border only with summer flowers;
or where there is an accomplished artist, with
consummate taste and skill, with ample accommodation and abundant material, it must be delightful to realise such masses of bloom, such contrasts
of colour and of form as those described and
delineated by Miss Jekyll and Mr. Selfe-Leonard
in the *Journal of the Royal Horticultural Society*
for April 1898; but for those who have neither
the science nor the supplies, I think that a mixed
collection, planted according to knowledge with
reference to size and colour, would give the
larger amount of pleasure.

When the Christmas Roses (with a couple of
hand-glasses to preserve their purity of colour
from the frost and rain) are gone we have the
lovely winter blooming *Iris, Stylosa (Unguicularis)
alba, purpurea, Speciosa, Histrioides, Bakeriana,* and
Reticulata, the latter gleaming, like the cohorts of

the Assyrians, "in purple and gold," the yellow Jasmine, the *Cheimonanthus fragrans*, and the *Narcissus*, and all the bulbs following their herald *Chionodoxa*, who has raised his head above the snow to tell us about the glory of the coming spring; and then there is all the summer sheen until we come to the *Anemone Japonica* and the *Asters* and the hardy *Chrysanthemums*, and to the *Christmas Rose* once more.

What is the history of the origin and the development of the Herbaceous Border? When the novelty and the fascination of the gay plants from the greenhouse began to subside, when the excitement was followed by the usual reaction—I must not say when retribution travelled on the track of crime—when the gardener began to count the loss and gain, and, when his eyes were aching with the monotonous glare, to apprehend that he who feasts every day feasts no day, or rather that it was better to have wholesome food throughout the year than dainties highly seasoned for three or four months; when he began to meditate upon his old favourites and to mourn their absence; when the desire came to dethrone the usurper, and the vow was made, "the king shall have his own again"; he was perplexed a while by the question, where will you receive the exiles? where will you prepare the throne? They would be altogether incompatible in the position chosen, and in the geometrical beds prepared for "bedding out." It was short and easy work to destroy, to dig up and cut down, to efface and transform, but to restore and replace was a *magnum opus*, which could only be laborious and long. The beginnings were minute, the process was slow, so slow that to this day I know countless gardens in which the beds are chiefly occupied by the same summer flowers (in many cases near to towns supplied by the nurseryman), and no real attempt is made to grow hardy shrubs or flowers.

By degrees, notwithstanding, the outcasts made a reappearance. Here and there on the borders and in corners of the pleasure ground, and yet more largely in the kitchen garden. The little groups in front of the espalier apples and pears grew larger until they touched each other, and formed the Herbaceous Border.

The first successful example which I remember was that which is mentioned by Mr. Robinson

in his "English Flower Garden," and which was
formed by my friend Mr. Frank Miles in the
Rectory garden at Bingham, Notts. Frank in-
herited from his mother (one of the most accomplished and beautiful of women) his success in
art and his love of a garden; but his father,
who was an ideal parish priest of the George
Herbert and Keble type, was not horticultural.
"No son," Frank said, "ever had a more affec-
tionate father, but, out of his intense desire to
help everybody, he will go about the garden
with a hoe, and his want of discrimination
between flowers and weeds is at times disastrous. I have twice found a plant which I
must own has a mean appearance, but is nevertheless a treasure, lying on its back with its
toes, I mean its roots, in the air. I erected a
large cardboard notice : 'No weeds in this
border—all trespassers will be prosecuted.' He
read it with a beautiful smile, but he went
elsewhere with his hoe."

I recall other horticultural associations between
those nearest akin, which were more harmonious.
I was walking in a garden with a lady, whose
daughter had made it one of the most attractive

and interesting in the land, and I said, "You must take a most happy interest in all this charming work?"—and she made answer, "I am allowed to pay the wages, and weed."

I had a friend, a man of ability and culture, a sportsman, and yet such an abject slave of his pretty young bride that you expected him on certain occasions to fall and grovel at her feet. How nearly he approached such a prostration you will learn from a conversation which I now repeat. Knowing that his wife was an enthusiastic florist, I inquired—

"Do you do much in the garden?"

"Oh yes, a good deal."

"What sort of good deal?"

"I weed."

"Do you? then you are much more learned than I thought. Your wife is an expert, and would not allow you to weed unless she was quite sure that you would not make mistakes."

"I only weed the drive and the walks at present."

"Do you like it?"

"Oh yes. My wife has given me the blade of an old oyster-knife and a bit of carpet to kneel on, and, when the oyster-knife does not come in contact with the larger lumps of gravel, the hours pass sweetly away."

"Do you do anything else?"

"Yes, I carry the basket, you know, with the pruning-knife, and the scissors, and the tallies, and the bast."

"What is the bast?"

"The matting, with which we tie the twigs."

"Is that all you do?"

"Oh dear no! I wheel the barrow with the soil for planting, and the sand, and the trowel, and the artificial manure. And then in the evening I propel that beas—I mean that admirable zinc tub, with the water flopping over the side!"

The following selection which I have made of plants suitable for the foundation of a Herbaceous Border, with their height, colour, and time of flowering, may be helpful to the young gardeners for whom I write.

LIST OF PLANTS FOR HERBACEOUS BORDER

NAME.	HEIGHT.	COLOUR.	TIME OF FLOWERING.
Achillea	6 in. to 6 ft.	White and yellow.	June.
Adonis	1 foot.	Yellow.	March.
Alyssum	9 inches.	Yellow.	April.
Anemone, including Japonica . . .	6 to 1 foot.	All colours.	March to October.
Anthemis tinctoria . .	1½ foot.	Pale yellow.	June.
Antirrhinum	1½ foot.	Various.	June.
Aquilegia	1½ foot.	Various.	June.
Arabislucida variegata .	9 inches.	White.	April.
Aster	2 to 3 feet.	Violet and reddish purple.	September.
Aubrietia	6 inches.	Violet.	April.
Campanula	5 in. to 4 ft.	Blue, purple, and white.	June.
Carnations and pinks .	1 foot.	Various.	July.
Cheiranthus	1 to 2 feet.	Yellow and red.	April.
Chrysanthemums . .	3 feet.	Various.	November
Crocus	6 inches.	Yellow, purple, and white.	February
Delphinium	2 to 9 feet.	Blue, purple, and red.	June.
Diclytra	2 feet.	Pink.	May.
Dictamnus Fraxinella .	2 feet.	Purple.	July.
Digitalis	3 feet.	Various.	July.
Dodecatheon	1 foot.	White, purple, and rose.	May.
Doronicum	2 feet.	Yellow.	April.
Echinops	2 feet.	Blue and white.	July.
Epimedium	6 to 12 in.	White, yellow, and red.	June.
Eremurus	5 to 8 feet.	Yellow, white, and pink.	June.
Erigeron	1 foot.	Purple, white, yellow, blue.	July.
Eryngium	2½ feet.	Blue.	June.
Gaillardia	1 foot.	Yellow and orange.	July.
Gentian	8 inches.	Purple.	July.
Geranium, Cranesbill .	1½ foot.	Pink and purple.	July.

L

PLANTS FOR HERBACEOUS BORDER (*continued*)

NAME.	HEIGHT.	COLOUR.	TIME OF FLOWERING.
Geum	1½ foot.	Scarlet.	July.
Gladiolus	3 feet.	Various.	Aug. & Sept.
Gypsophila	3 feet.	White.	July.
Harpalium	2 feet.	Yellow.	July.
Helianthus	3 to 8 feet.	Yellow.	August.
Hemerocallis	3 feet.	Yellow.	June.
Heuchara	8 inches.	Rose.	June.
Hyacinths	6 inches.	Various.	April.
Hyacinthus candicans .	4 feet.	White.	July.
Hydrangea	3 feet.	{ White, pink, and pale blue }	July.
Indigofera	3 feet.	Rose.	July.
Inula	2 feet.	Yellow.	July.
Iris	4 in. to 4 ft.	All colours.	Nov. to Sept.
Knipholia	5 feet.	Red and orange.	August.
Leucojum vernum . .	6 inches.	White.	April.
Lilies	6 in. to 10 ft.	All colours.	April to June.
Lupin	3 feet.	Blue.	June.
Lychnis	2 feet.	Brilliant red.	June.
Montbretia	1 foot.	Yellow, vermilion.	July.
Narcissus	1 foot.	Various.	March.
Œnothera	1½ foot.	Yellow.	June.
Omphalodes	1 foot.	Dark blue.	June.
Orobus Vernus . . .	1 foot.	Purple.	March.
Pæonia	1½ foot.	Various.	June.
Pancratium	2 feet.	White.	July.
Papaver	6 in. to 3 ft.	Various.	June.
Penstemon	1 foot.	Various.	July.
Phlox	3 feet.	Various.	July.
Polygonatum	2 feet.	White.	May.
Pyrethrum	2 feet.	White, carmine.	May.
Romneya Coultheri .	6 feet.	White.	June.
Rudbeckia	2 to 5 feet.	Yellow and pink.	July.
Spiræa	3 feet.	{ White, red, and crimson. }	June.
Staticé	2½ feet.	Blue.	July.
Tulips	10 to 12 in.	All colours.	April.
Verbascum	4 feet.	Yellow.	July.

The front of this border should be edged, *in undulating lines,* with the Alpine and other dwarf plants which I have chosen (see page 149) to surround the large beds adjoining, and these should be also intermixed with the low stones, which add so much to their beauty by contrast, shelter, and support. With this addition the list for the Herbaceous Border will include one hundred varieties, and as some of these may be advantageously planted in groups, and as there will probably be a subsequent introduction of Cannas or Dahlias, the collection, though capable of improvement, will furnish (if it is not profane to associate flowers with furniture) a great extent of ground, and will not fail to please the collector. There may be many omissions; some I have made purposely, not having discovered the charms or the hardihood which others have proclaimed; some I may have forgotten, but if any of the latter are of real excellence, I shall soon hear of it from the kindly critic, who is waiting to announce that the author "must have been bereft of his senses," or "could never have seen a decent garden," who did not include plants — — — in his catalogue; just

as when we have visited a gallery of pictures
some friend, on finding that we failed to notice
Smith's portrait of Jones, rejoices to assure us
that we have missed the gem of the collection.

Behind the Herbaceous Border there should
be a strong screen of larch or other wood,
about eight feet in height, so arranged as to
allow the winds a free circulation among the
flowers without visiting their cheeks too roughly.
This fence should be covered with *Clematis*,
Montana, Jackmanni, and other hardy varieties;
Cydonias; *Weigela Rosea*, trained on the wood;
Ceanothus, Gloire de Versailles (to be well
mulched through the winter); *Passiflora*, Constance Elliott (to have similar treatment); *Jasmines*
and *Honeysuckles*; but chiefly *Roses*, Crimson
Rambler, Madame Alfred Carriere, Bouquet
d'or, Ulrich Brunner, Gloire de Dijon, Duke of
Edinburgh, Blairii 2, Madame Isaac Perriere,
Felicité Perpetué, Charles Lawson, Madame
Berard, Reine Marie Henriette, Climbing Cap-
tain Christy, W. A. Richardson, Longworth
Rambler, Carmine Pillar, Madame D'Arblay,
the Garland, and Reine Olga de Wurtenberg.

There should be a broad gravel walk in

front of the Herbaceous Border, not only for the tender and delicate women among us, who will not set the sole of their feet upon the grass, but as a general promenade in times of dew or rain, and for the convenience of the gardener. On the further side of this walk I see no escape from the objectionable straight line, but the beds on the one hand and the border on the other should occupy the attention of the visitor and divert his eye from this sad distress. The introduction of such plants as would grow at intervals over the walk, and so break the monotony, would detract from the effect of both the border and the beds, and would bring unnecessary embarrassments to the operations of the mowing machine. Let us go to "fields fresh and pastures new," through the main garden and shrubbery, and over the lawn, to

CHAPTER
VIII

The Rose
Garden

"Le lion est toujours le roi des animaux, l'aigle le monarque des airs, et la Rose la Reine des fleurs."
—Redouté.

"The Rose is, in addition to other merits, an English flower, almost an English institution, and I am glad you have made it the subject of special study and commemoration."—(*From a letter written by the* Right Hon. W. E. Gladstone *to the author, March 28,* 1877.)

I HAVE recommended the frequent introduction of Roses on the walls of the house, in the beds of the greater garden, and on the screen of the herbaceous border, but this beautiful flower has such a pre-eminence and diversity that it should have in addition, wherever it is possible, a garden of its own. No other flower can show such a compass of colour and form, and no reply has been received to the question, which George Herbert asked more than two hundred and fifty years ago, " What is sweeter than a rose ? " Where shall we find such a variety in size, as between tiny *Cecile* and huge *Ulrich Brunner*, between *Her Majesty* and *Perle d'or ?* in growth, between *Little Gem* and *Rampant?* in colour, between *Marguerite Dickson* and *Charles Lefebvre*, *Marechal Niel* and *Prince Camile de Rohan ?* Or where shall we find a flower with such a continuous bloom ? where such munificence as the Royal Bounty of the Rose ? There is no other claimant to the title of *Semper florens*, bestowed by an œcumenical council of botanists upon the *China* or *monthly Roses*—" Semper, ubique, ab omnibus "—always, everywhere, for all. *Gloire de Dijon* flowers upon our walls in May, and brings out new editions until the end of the year. " The time of Roses " is from June until there comes " a nipping frost," and in this year of 1899, and in the second week of January, I had a very pretty flower of *La France !*

The Rose Garden must be a garden of Roses only. We do not plant shrubs around our oaks, and no birds may warble when the nightingale sings. It is the palace of the queen, and though she rejoices in the society of her subjects elsewhere, she brooks no rival near her throne. I sometimes see round holes in grass plots, generally by the side of walks in order to attract especial notice, in straight lines and at measured intervals, with a long stick rising from the centre, supporting a rose-bush of irregular dimensions, and in a condition, more or less, of morbid debility. There is nothing at all like it in the natural world; and as if to add insult to injury, and as though it were not enough to expose this lanky, top-heavy excrescence to all the winds of heaven, the cavity below is filled with a miscellaneous collection of remnants, to intercept the nourishment so sorely needed by the invalid upstairs. I have remonstrated with the proprietor, but when he told me that he " was under the impression that all the best roses grew like that, and that he had not noticed the other things," I abstained from discussion.

I am painfully aware that I differ in this matter from an illustrious gardener and author, who is my dear friend, with whom I believe myself to be in full sympathy as to all the great principles of horticulture, and who has written in his *magnum opus*[1] that he " covers his rose-beds with pansies, violets, stonecrops, rock-foils, thymes, and " (here comes the unkindest cut of all) " any little rock plants to spare. Carpeting these rose-beds with life and beauty was half the battle." But there is no occasion for half a battle, though it be a *bataille des fleurs*, nor for contest or comparison of any kind. We do not wish to have our attention diverted, our homage divided, by carpets, however lovely and attractive; and though good roses may be grown with these additions, better roses may be grown without them. If the beds are not sufficiently covered by the taller varieties, why not plant some of lesser growth, such as the lovely *Princess de Sagan*, or make a selection of Roses suitable for pegging-down? If there might be any special dispensation for the addition of other flowers, it would be only conceded in small

[1] The English Flower Garden.

gardens, or where the surroundings were adverse to the cultivation of Roses, and then exclusively to the bulbs which precede, or to the annuals which follow, the royal efflorescence.

Even in the Riviera, where the depth of rich soil below and the bright sun above might be pleaded for the mixture of other flowers with the Rose, so far as their sustentation is concerned, no such interference is permitted. Lord Brougham, who has a splendid garden of Roses at Cannes, warns us "not to allow grass or flowering plants to be in their immediate vicinity, because these, acting as leeches, draw from the ground the very ingredients that are required for the life-blood of the Rose."

"And who are you," I hear the critic say, " with your

> 'I am Sir Oracle, and when I speak
> Let no dog bark' ?

Who made you Lord Chamberlain to the Queen of Flowers?" I make answer—because he who would guide others must show his credentials—"If you please, Mr. Critic, I am the man who invented Rose Shows, and won many cups, and wrote a book about Roses,

and am the President of the National Rose
Society; and for fifty-four years I have admired
and studied the Rose." If the critic intimates,
not for the first time, that I have wasted this
portion of my life and dishonoured my sacred
vocation by these diversions, I lose all sense of
humility, boldly proclaiming that I have not
only derived from horticulture great help and
refreshment in my work, but, brought up among
horses, hounds, and partridges, I have from
boyhood to middle age occasionally enjoyed the
sports of the field; and that as regards my mini-
strations in a small country parish, I always
maintained the daily service of the Church, and
my daily visits to the school; knew every man,
woman, and child in the place, and have preached,
since I took Orders, in 500 churches from the
the Land's End to the Border. This is rank
egotism, but it is provoked by rank ignorance,
and when the captious Puritan, who can hardly
distinguish between a pæony and a rose, whom
no gold could induce to ride at a stile, before
whose gun the full-grown pheasant might leis-
urely and without peril pursue his onward flight,
denounces recreations which he cannot share,

there comes a crisis of cruelty, which is resented
by the proverbial worm, and evokes a protest
even from a Dean—

"Semper ego auditor tantum, nunquamne reponam ?"

I must confess that on one occasion my zealous
loyalty for her majesty the Rose led me into
error so ridiculous that I was constrained to
present it, although I might have kept it to
myself, for the mirthful enjoyment of my
friends. I was requested by the chairman at
a great city dinner to propose "the Visitors,"
with a special reference to some of his guests
from France. While I was speaking I saw on
the opposite side of the table an elderly gentleman of imposing appearance, having his hair
close cut with the exception of an enormous
white moustache. He wore over his breast a
broad crimson ribbon, and I said to myself,
"That's a Maréchal of France!" Accordingly,
when I had disposed of my fellow-countrymen
by assuring them of the joy and honour of their
presence (I was a visitor also, and it seemed
like a glorification of our noble selves, but the
chairman declined to entertain the objection), I

proceeded to welcome our friends from France with a polite bow to the Maréchal, and finally expressed my special sympathies as a Rosarian indebted to France for the introduction of our most beautiful Roses. "It is no exaggeration to say," I concluded, turning with a sweet smile to the Maréchal, "that 'La Rose est la Reine des fleurs et la France est la Reine des Roses.'" I sat down, and inquired the name and title of the illustrious soldier, and was told that he was a London pawnbroker, wearing his badge of office, as President of a Benevolent Society.

The Rose Garden must not be in an exposed situation. It must have shelter, but it must not have shade. No boughs may darken, no drip may saturate, no roots may rob, the Rose. Screens there should be to resist rude Boreas, breakwaters to the haven, but not near enough to intercept the sunshine or the free circulation of air. They rejoice in that sunshine, and should have what there is to be had of it in this our cloudy land, I believe E.S.E. to be the best aspect for Roses, so manifest is the influence of the rising and midday sun.

The faith which sang

> " Once again I was rising before the sun,
>   For in childhood I was told,
> If its early ray on my head should fall
>   'Twould turn each lock to gold "

might realise a disappointment as to the aureole; but the same happy result would come to the child as to the flowers, from these interviews with " Phœbus" when he " 'gins to rise," that is, a rosy complexion.

In our ideal garden, the entrance to the Rosary is either from the lawn between the shrubberies, or from the terrace walk down the steps, but such arrangements must vary in accordance with the formation and surroundings of the beds. There can be no more beautiful approach than the pergola, which is before the reader, and which was covered, when I saw it, with " *the Crimson Rambler,*" with Tea roses on either side. In some convenient corner of the Rose Garden there should be a bower, boarded and roofed and floored, with seats and table, containing drawers for catalogues and tools, and a cupboard for the crockery of five o'clock tea.

On the east side of the Rose Garden the

PERGOLA AT PENRHYN CASTLE

shrubbery, through which we enter it, will be a sufficient protection; at the south end, between the Rose and the Rock gardens, a hedge of Japanese *Rosa Rugosa*,[1] red and white intermixed, charming with its early flowers, and afterwards with its beautiful fruit; and on the western, pillars or a pergola.

Roses should be grown in rich loam, or in fertile clay well drained. With a mixture of lighter soil, burnt earth, leaf mould, "top-spit" of old pasture, and liberally enriched with farm-yard manure, Roses will grow, if they are well cared for, where growth is possible, but they will not flourish where they are overshadowed, overcrowded, smoked, or starved. Personally, I have good reasons to prefer the clay, in which, all around my ancestral home, luxuriates the wild rose, the parent stock of so many scions, who have won victories for me in the wars of the Roses. Very charming, those exhibition flowers, but not to be compared with the bowers of beauty which almost met over some of our "occupation roads," lanes made for the farmers' use, in the olden time before the land

[1] The Scotch Roses and the Sweet Briars make charming hedges.

was shaven and shorn, and no man had ever heard of that disgusting abomination, the prickwire fence.

The walks should be entirely of grass, and, where it is closely mown and well rolled, it is always available as a dry and delightful promenade for those persons who do not prefer wet weather for the enjoyment of their love among the Roses, and would regard it as disrespectful to appear in goloshes before the queen of flowers. We do not wish to see them when they are battered by heavy rains, and I have never overcome my regret that a gentleman of Mr. Cowper's poetic ability should have recorded the injudicious behaviour of Mary in conveying a rose to Anna, which had only just been washed by a shower, and

> "Unfit as it was
> For a nosegay, so dripping and drowned."

It is of all times the worst for gathering Roses when

> "The plentiful moisture encumbers the flower,
> And weighs down its beautiful head."

No mother would bring her pretty child into the drawing-room, when it "had been washed, just washed," in its tub, or when the tears were glisten-

ing on its sweet little face (after furious but
ineffectual efforts to kick the under-nurse).   And
why does Mr. Cowper suddenly appear upon the
scene to grab at the Rose, and

> " Swinging it rudely, too rudely alas,
>   He snapped it—it fell to the ground."

We read the history with mingled feelings, pity
for the ignorance of Mary, resentment for the
impetuosity of the poet, sorrow for the bereavement of Anne.

These walks must be broad in proportion to the
beds, as in the Great Garden.   There is no frame
so appropriate as the grass for the most beautiful
of all pictures, the flowers.

The Rosarium must include all the manifold
varieties of the Rose.   On the western side of the
shrubbery, which separates it from the lawn, the
vigorous Ayrshire and Sempervirens Roses, secured
to strong poles eight or ten feet in height, might
appear in the foreground as introductory heralds
and ushers, and in the verandah or pergola the
climbing varieties selected for the walls of the
house.   These, with the addition of the Roses
commended for the screen behind the Herbaceous
Border, should also be planted within the Rosarium

M

on pillars and on arcades of larch or other wood. Timber is greatly to be preferred to iron, which has always a stiff, cold, artificial appearance. The metal may be more durable, but if the stout poles are charred, tarred, and set three feet deep in the ground, he who erects them will rarely live to see their fall. These pillars and arcades, where they have been tastefully arranged and are covered by a healthful growth, diversify and beautify the garden, but they require care in the choice and in the pruning. If for example *Blairii* 2, one of the loveliest summer Roses in cultivation, is closely cut, it will be as a barren fig-tree, *ficulnus inutile lignum*, all foliage and no flowers; and yet the knife is needed from time to time to shorten some of the lower shoots, or you will have an unsuccessful blank below. The fact is that Roses like Rosarians have different habits, and require that difference of treatment which is only revealed to study and experience. If you wish for Roses few and large, you must prune within four " eyes " of the main stock : if you desire a larger quantity smaller in size, you may leave five or six of these dormant buds. In all cases the weak growth and that which is decayed must be removed.

The Arcade, being on a much larger scale, will require yet more consideration and culture. Whether the arch above be pointed or round, I would advise that it should not be placed on the upright posts before it is required to support the rose. Even to those who soon forget the ugliness of the scaffold in their foresight of the fair edifice which it helps to build, the bare poles are a trial of faith, and when these are surmounted by a construction as nude and desolate as their own, we are vexed by obtrusive thoughts of the gymnasium with its swings and trapezes, and we might add, as the Greek word suggests, with the scanty clothing of the athletes.

The design of the Rose Garden, the number and size of the beds, depends upon the space to be occupied. If there is the ambition and the opportunity, the site, the soil, and the balance at the bank, to represent in its fulness the beauty of the royal flower, I would suggest that every variety selected for cultivation should form a separate group in a bed containing not less than twelve plants.

This plan involves, of course, a large garden

and a large outlay, but it may be easily reduced, not by diminishing the size of the beds, but by planting two, three, or four varieties in a bed.

If a minimum of ground and expenditure is necessary, the beds must be larger, and there must be a general assembly, with this restriction, the Hybrid Perpetuals, the Hybrid Teas, and the Teas should be in separate groups.

I submit, accordingly, two suggestive designs, the first, very kindly lent to me by Lady Falmouth, of her most charming garden at Mereworth, and the second a plan of the Rosarium at the Swanley Horticultural College, which was sent to me for approbation, and has been completed and planned in accordance with my advice.

The simpler the arrangement the better, but there must be broad grass walks between the beds and a broad margin of grass surrounding the whole. The convenience of the mower, and the size of the machine, must have due consideration, and for the same object, the roses must not be planted too near the boundaries of the beds.

At the same time, arrangements can be easily
made to prevent an unsightly interval of soil,
hiatus valde deflendus, between the plants and
the sward.

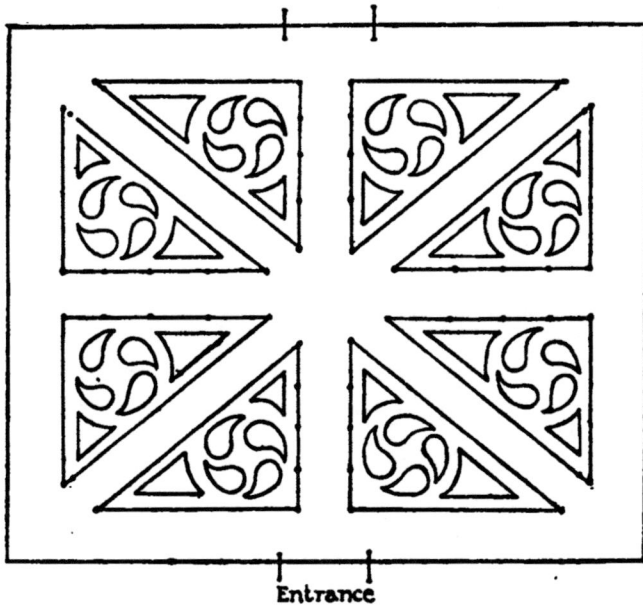

Entrance

Plan of·Rosary·at·Mereworth·Castle·

To these plans is added a list of the most
beautiful Roses, which may be relied upon for
their vigorous growth.   There is a multitude of
other Roses not quite so attractive or so hardy,

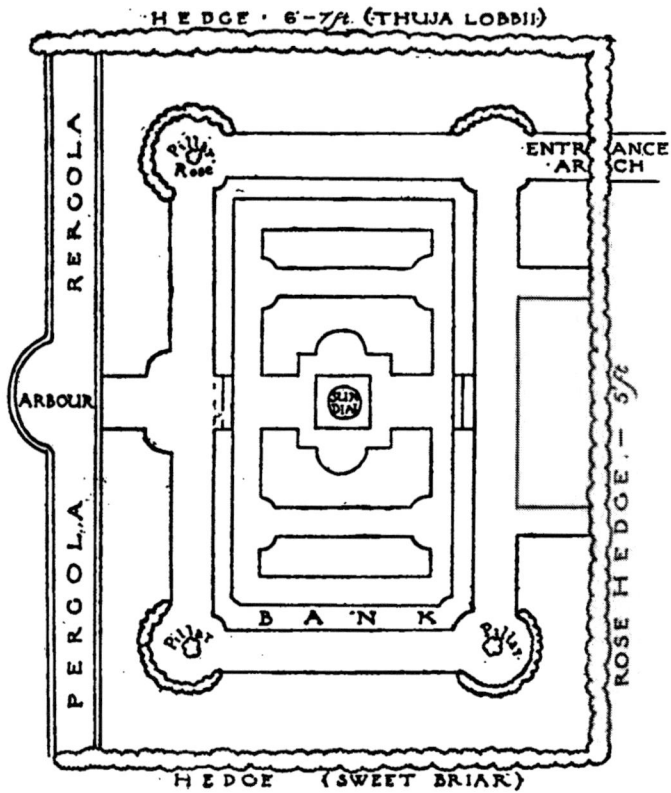

Plan of ROSE GARDEN at the HORTICULTURAL COLLEGE, SWANLEY, KENT.

which deserve a place in our gardens, and will be found in the nurseries.[1]

Hybrid Perpetuals

Baroness Rothschild.
Charles Lefebvre.
Doctor Andry.
Duke of Edinburgh.
Etienne Levet.
General Jacqueminot.
Her Majesty.
Louis Van Houtte.
Madame Gabriel Luizet.
Margaret Dickson.
Marie Baumann.
Merveille de Lyon.
Mrs. John Laing.
Ulrich Brunner.

Hybrid Teas

Augustine Guinoisseau.
Bardon Job.
Captain Christy.
Caroline Testout.

Gloire Lyonnaise.
Grace Darling.
Gustave Regis.
Lady Mary Fitzwilliam.
La France.
Madame Pernet Ducher.
Marquis of Salisbury.
Mrs. W. J. Grant.[2]
Papa Gontier.
Viscountess Folkestone.

Teas

Anna Ollivier.
Beauté Inconstante.
Catherine Mermet.
Comtesse de Nadaillac.
Dr. Grill.
Ernest Metz.
Francisca Kruger.
General Shablekine.[3]
George Nabonnaud.

---

[1] The most complete list of Roses is "The Official Catalogue of the National Rose Society." The secretaries are the Rev. H. H. D'Ombrain, Westwell Vicarage, Ashford, Kent, and E. Mawley, Esq., Rose Bank, Berkhampsted, Herts.

[2] This exquisite rose was sent to me under the name of "La Belle Siebricht," by Messrs. Siebricht of New York, when I was in that city in 1895.

[3] This rose is not in our English catalogues, and must be procured from the raiser, Mons. Nabonnaud, Grasse, Cannes, Nice, France. Lord Brougham describes it as " caring neither for cold, damp, sun, or mildew "; and he declares " that if a law was passed that one man

Homére.
Hon. Edith Gifford.
Innocente Pirola.
Jean Ducher.
Ma Capucine.
Madam Bravy.
Madame de Watteville.
Madame Falcot.
Madame Hoste.
Madame Lambard.
Maman Cochet.
Marie Van Houtte.
Perle des Jardins.
Princesse de Sagan.
Rubens.
Souvenir d'Elise.
Souvenir d'un ami.
Souvenir de S. A. Prince.
The Bride.

China
Laurette Messimy.

Polyantha
Cecile Brunner.
Perle d'or.
Reine des Polyanthas.

Moss
The Common.
Laneii.
Little Gem.

Provence
The Common, "Old
Cabbage."

Bourbon
Madame Isaac Pereire.
Souvenir de la Malmaison.

Austrian Briar Roses
Austrian Copper.
Harrisonii.
Persian Yellow.

Sweet Briars
Common.
Janet's Pride.
Lord Penzance's Varieties.

Scotch
In variety.

should cultivate but one variety of rose, he should without hesitation choose General Shablekine, as being without a rival, flowering continuously, with 100 blooms of equal merit on a plant. Its constitution and hardiness would guarantee it success in our colder climate, and of all roses it is the most faithful and generous." Without disparaging the merits of the General, one could have wished that the flower had received a more euphonious title. The rose by any other name would have smelt as sweetly.

In making this list I have lingered from time to time with a sorrowful spirit over the names of Roses which once held a royal supremacy, but have been superseded by others of a similar type, but of a more perfect form and colour— *O matre pulchrâ filia pulchrior !*—or which seem to have deteriorated in the quality or the constancy of their bloom; but most regretfully over those which still retain their pre-eminence, but which we cannot grow out of doors in England with any certain success. Of these *Chromatella*, or *Cloth of Gold* (by some regarded as distinct, but generally considered to be identical) is acknowledged by the Rosarians, who have seen it in its perfection, to take the precedence in form and colour of all the Roses! Round and deep, each flower resembles such a chalice of pure gold as Hebe might have presented to the gods. Alas, it cannot endure our gloom, and damp, and frost (it is gratifying to know that on our empire the sun never sets, but the joy would be greatly increased if it would rise occasionally at home), and I have only seen it once growing vigorously on English ground, fifty years ago, on the wall of a cottage in the village of Carlton-on-Trent, and once exhibited from the neighbourhood of Colchester at one of our National Shows. Even in the Riviera, where I have seen it covering long distances of high walls, and producing its long branches and lovely roses from the summit and centre of great timber trees, it has been so hacked and mangled by tourists and purveyors, that it seems to languish under persecution, and to be impaired both in abundance and beauty. Here and there, we are told, "far from the madding crowd," it retains its ancient glory, but I can testify that in the more frequented parts of the Riviera its angel visits are few and far between. *Maréchal Niel*—no rose ever produced such a sensation as this, the grandest of its colour, when it was sent to us from France some thirty-five years ago—may be grown on a warm wall looking east or south, and the largest flowers which I have ever achieved have been those which have been so treated, but we must have propitious seasons to secure such a consummation, and its size prevents a thorough protection from the extreme severities of an English winter. Under glass it delights us with a marvellous luxuriance of flower and foliage, and, hanging over our heads from the roof, gives us the complete enjoyment of its beauty.

Many years ago (these anecdotes will obtrude) I had a charming friend, whose name was Marshall. Being in Paris in the days of the Empire, he went to a reception at the Tuileries. He gave his name on entrance as Mons. Marshall, but was amazed, as he passed into the Grand Salon, to hear himself announced as *Monsieur Le Maréchal!* and was even more perturbed in his mind, when, reflected in one of the huge mirrors, he saw that one of his scarlet braces, detached from one of its buttons, and from his waistcoat, was swinging to and fro at his side. He told us that he found some comfort in the fact that the appendage was evidently regarded as an order of distinguished merit, and that the spectators may have imagined a close connection between the Knights of the Brace and the Garter.

Niphetos, the largest and loveliest of our pure white roses, may also be grown on a wall, when well mulched in winter (and all roses, especially Tea roses, should be well mulched in winter), but a prolonged and bitter frost will be more or less disastrous; whereas there is no rose in a conservatory which grows or flowers more freely.

I have grown *Fortune's Yellow* for many years on the walls of my house in Notts, and as it still makes me small offerings of its pretty blooms, I cannot cut it down; but when I recall its capabilities, as revealed, for example, over a large pergola in Doctor Bennett's garden at Mentone, I am conscious that it is the right rose in the wrong place, that it should be under protection, and that some stronger substitute should occupy its place.

Like dewdrops from the rose when the sun is up, these little disappointments of the Rosarian vanish, and he feels only shame for his regrets, when in the time of roses he surveys the scene around, and knows that in all the world there is not a fairer sight. More than this, that each succeeding year will add new treasures to his store. When it was my privilege to suggest and organise the first great national show of roses only, in the year 1858, there were but six of those flowers which are now deemed worthy of exhibition, namely, *Devoniensis* (1838), *Niphetos* (1844), *Madame Willermoz* (1845), *Souvenir d'un ami* (1846), *Madame Bravy* (1848), and *General Jacqueminot* (1853). We had a large assortment of Hybrid Perpetuals, Gallicas, Hybrid Chinas, and Bourbons, with names still dear to us, though the modern Rosarian never heard them; and they had a special beauty of their own, and their size and their colour made them peerless in our sight and absorbed all our powers of admiration. Can the roses at the Crystal Palace do more?

Many roses of exquisite beauty have been introduced such as those, which I have enumerated, in the Hybrid Perpetual division since the first of our National Shows, *Charles Lefebvre* in 1861, *Marie Baumann* in 1863, and *Mrs. John Laing* in 1887; but our great acquisition has been in those Tea and Hybrid Tea roses, which have a symmetrical grace and a delicate refinement of colour not found elsewhere. *La France* is the head of the latter family, and when we consider all the qualities of this rose, its size, shape, colour, fragrance, and continuous bloom, it seems to take precedence over all. There are others which may for a time contest the supremacy, but *La France* has staying powers which in horses and athletes win the race. It is not only "the last rose of summer," but the last and best of autumn. I have named her lovely companions, and for three of these, *Grace Darling*, *Lady Mary Fitzwilliam*, and *Viscountess Folkestone*, we are indebted to the late Mr. Bennett, the champion raiser of English roses, and to him we also owe *Mrs. John Laing*, *Hybrid Perpetual*, his masterpiece, and that magnificent rose, which, seen at its best, well deserves its illustrious title, *Her Majesty*.

Of the *Teas* what shall I say? Neither words nor pictures can do them justice. I told Sir John Millais, with the impudence of an old friend, that he could not paint a rose. He replied, "I can reproduce that which I see"; and then he added, "but you know too much about roses." I took this as an admission that there might be more to see than he saw. There are some roses, especially the single varieties, which Redouté painted with such consummate skill, whose portraits please in the absence of the original, but as a rule they are failures, and it seems as though the more beautiful the flower, as for example *Comtesse de Nadaillac, Madame de Watteville*, and *Princesse de Sagan*, the greater the disappointment.

I have been asked by young Rosarians whether I should advise them to exhibit, and I have given them the answer of my cautious gardener, "It depends." In the first place, as the founder of Rose Shows, and for many years an exhibitor and judge, I hold a brief as counsel for the defence against those who denounce them as interfering with the general cultivation of garden roses for the sake of monster blooms, comparatively few, which have been condemned as the results of a triple alliance, pride, avarice, and farmyard manure. I have noticed that these objections have been frequently urged by persons who, from deficiency of soil, enthusiasm, or knowledge, have failed to realise the rose in its full completeness, or by those who have exhibited without attracting the sympathies of the judge, and have come home depressed and sore, like knights from a tournament who have been unhorsed and rolled in the dust.

Rose Shows have added largely to the number

of Rosarians and to the improvement of roses, and now that they include every variety of the flower, single and double, the best specimens of the old and the new, there could not be a more attractive or instructive source of information. And this feast of Roses is most

"Delectable, both to behold and taste,"

when we not only enjoy but promote its success. I know from experience the delight of cutting and arranging twenty-four or forty-eight faultless flowers, conveying them over one hundred miles of road and rail, and finally finding a card with "First Prize" written thereon in front of the collection.

Nevertheless, I reply again to the question, Do you advise me to exhibit?—"It depends." You must have a soil which seems to produce the rose spontaneously, as though the two loved each other ("I am not the rose," said the perfumed earth in the Persian fable, "but cherish me, for we have dwelt together"), with long clean shoots, and glossy foliage, and bright abundance of flowers; you must grow roses by the thousand, partly in your garden, and partly on budded

briars outside.   You must know the names,
habits, and position of every rose which you possess ; you must not shrink from rising at 3 A.M.
nor from travelling through the night; you
must not allow your favourites to monopolise
your ground to the exclusion of roses which you
cannot show, and of other beautiful flowers—if
you do, you are no true gardener ; whatever may
be your success, you must anticipate defeat when
the date of the Show is too early or too late
for your best display; when the judges, as in districts where experts are few, may be incompetent
persons ; and when the time comes, as sooner or
later come it will, in which some new competitor
shall bring the more vigorous growth of a virgin
soil with triumphant issues to the Show.   If
under these conditions, and with these anticipations, you resolve to exhibit ; if like young Norval
among the Grampian hills you have heard of
battles, of the Wars of the Roses, and have determined to fight; then let us hope that

> " Wheresoe'er thou move, good luck
> Shall fling her old shoe after."

If you succeed, be thankful.   If you fail,

> " Cromwell, I charge thee fling away ambition,"

N

and remember Luther's message, "Tell Philip Melanchthon, to leave off thinking that he's going to rule the world," and enjoy your roses, large and small, in all their beautiful diversity, at home.

CHAPTER IX
The Rock Garden

*"Of all forms of cultivating flowers rock gardening
is the most fascinating. Within a small space you may
grow innumerable dainty plants, which would be swallowed
up or would not thrive in the border—delicate Alpines,
little creeping vines, cool mosses, rare orchids, and much
of the minute and charming flora of the woods and
mountains."*—ELLWANGER: *"The Garden's Story."*
"Sermons in Stones."—SHAKESPEARE.

IN their combination of novelty, beauty, and
general adaptation, the "Alpine Flowers," and
those which from their similarity are associated
with them, are, when carefully tended and
tastefully arranged among the stones, the most
charming visitors which have come in my time
(and I am coeval with the gardener who, when
asked his age, replied that he should soon be
an "octogeranium") to enhance our garden joys.

Not to evoke comparison, to suggest disparage-
ment, or to diminish our appreciation of the
favourites we have loved so long—not rivals
but allies, a great colony added to the empire,
a domain newly discovered, fair and fragrant
as Araby the blest, the Rock Garden is a modern
and distinct addition, a new departure. For
some years Alpine plants were grown in pots,
plunged in ashes, and protected in glazed frames
during the winter months. Between thirty and
forty years ago, Mr. James M'Nab, the excellent Curator of the Royal Botanic Garden at
Edinburgh, utilised the stones of an old wall
which was taken down in the grounds, and
constructed a Rock Garden, which he divided
into uniform sections, separated by stone paths
and steps. These sections were then divided
into angular compartments of various sizes, and
each filled with soils suited for the various
plants that were to be put into them. Although the *tout ensemble* was monotonous, and
the numerous tallies suggested a Liliputian
cemetery, it was a most interesting collection
and a grand commencement. The length when
I saw it, in the genial company of its construc-

THE ROCK GARDEN, KEW

tor, was 190 feet, by 85 in breadth, and the height 12 feet.   It contained many thousand plants.

Artists and experts have made since those days great progress in developing the beauty of the Rock Garden; they have shown us what to plant, and where, and how.   Successful achievements may be seen at Kew, in the nurseries of Messrs. Backhouse at York, and in many private collections.   Mr. Robinson has been foremost in this, as in so many other branches of hardy floriculture, to encourage and to teach, by his exhaustive volume on "Alpine Flowers" and his commentary in the "English Flower Garden"; but there is still a strange indifference among gardeners generally as to a system which has never disappointed those who have tried it. Either they do not believe, because they do not know the enjoyment, or they apprehend difficulties which do not exist.

There had been yearnings, in past years, an indistinct idea, a dim, very dim, prevision of a Rock Garden, a dream of dawn in the darkness; but when the morning came most of the dreamers closed their eyes, and sighed, "You

have roused me too soon, let me slumber again."
I remember the "Rockeries" of my boyhood,
atrocious structures of clinkers and gypsum, and
bottle ends, and oyster shells (the initials of
the artist in cockles on the walk adjoining), on
which the proprietor might have been deservedly
stretched, like Prometheus, and pecked by the
birds. Even such distinguished men as Loudon
gave their sanction to " plant rockworks, protu-
berant surfaces, or declivities irregularly covered
with rocky fragments, land-stones, conglome-
rated gravel ! vitrified bricks, vitrified scoriæ,
flints, shells, spar, or other earthy and hard
mineral bodies !" adding long lists of flowers
for ornamenting "aggregations of stones, flints,
scoriæ, formed in imitation of rocky surfaces,"
although constrained to add that "such works
are in general to be looked on more as scenes
of culture, than of design or picturesque beauty."
On the other side of the Atlantic the famous
nurseryman, Mr. Peter Henderson, suggests that
"purely artificial rockwork may be made by
clinkers from iron or other furnaces being dipped
in water lime or cement, which gives a pleasing
drab-colour to their grotesque shapes," and he

adds that "a rockery so formed, and planted
with flowers of bright colours, *even without any
pretensions to being natural*, is always an attractive
and interesting object." Such erections have
been rightly denounced as rubbish-heaps dex-
terously concealed, volcanic eruptions, abortive
earthquakes, &c. To complete and to crown
their ugliness, I have seen them surmounted
not only by miniature mill-sails, which, after
a few spasmodic efforts to show the direction
of the wind, declined to take further notice
even of the wildest storm, but by effigies, done
in plaster of Paris, of the illustrious dead; and
I remember two busts in particular, representing
Dante and Tasso, which a young Etonian, son
of the owner of the garden, prejudiced perhaps
against the Italian poets by his unsatisfactory
intercourse with Virgil and Horace, had embellished with all the freedom and originality
of youthful Art, enriching the countenance of
Tasso with a black eye, and concealing the
laurels of Dante under the broken brim of a
huge, discarded straw hat!

Herewith we have the first of our *Sermons in
Stones*; beware of sham and counterfeits; do

not daub with untempered mortar; do not cover bricks with cement, in the hope that your friends will believe them to be rocks; have nothing to do with tricks or with trash. In your character, as in your garden, let all be real—to thine own self be true. Make no pretence of sanctity, social, intellectual superiority. Despise "the tinsel clink of compliment," the accusation of the absent, all words that may do hurt.

The stones must be stones, and they must be placed, not on their sides, nor on their ends, like acrobats standing on their heads, but in their natural form, sunk a few inches in the ground, and with an abundance of congenial soil, loam, intermixed with sand and grit, around, within, and wherever they are situated, high or low. It is a fatal mistake to suppose that these small plants will flourish in a shallow soil. Many of them will make roots more than a foot in length, as tourists have discovered to their surprise, and to the trial of their patience, in their first efforts to transplant them from their native homes on the mountains. And far more numerously at home our gardeners have discovered too late the sad results of atrophy, that "evil is done

for want of thought," and that they have starved
these little ones to death.

And where shall we find such a vivid illustra-
tion of the Divine parable and sermon, so
familiar to us all, "some fell upon stony places,
where they had not much earth, and forthwith
they sprung up, because they had no deepness of
earth; and when the sun was up they were
scorched, and because they had no root they
withered away"?   Not only in its highest instruction, that we should be rooted and grounded in
our faith, which springs from the Rock, instead
of being carried about by every wind of doctrine,
like trees which, having their roots on the surface, are the first to go down in the storm; but,
descending to a lower level, we learn from this
Sermon in Stones to be more thorough and less
superficial, so that, instead of being everything
by turns and nothing long, a Jack-of-all-trades
and master of none, we may, by concentrating
our energies upon our special business, upon
special studies or accomplishments which are
most congenial to us, become masters who can
give orders with the authority of experience,
debaters who can speak with the confidence of

knowledge, artists not ashamed of their performances, because, so far as they go, they are in
accordance with the true principles of art; and
so, instead of being scorched and shrivelled when
they are exposed to the sunshine, the shining
light of wisdom and truth, they can rejoice in the
warmth and in the brightness so beneficent to the
good ground in which their roots lie deep.

"Whatsoever thy hand findeth to do, do it
with thy might." Even in our recreations we
should resolve to attain some height of excellence, rather than remain on a dead level or
become an all-round duffer. If a man cannot
ride to hounds, why does he buy hunters? If he
is perpetually missing, why does he carry a gun?
There is something which he can do well, if he
will try, and will take as his motto *quod facio,
valde facio*; and when by perseverance he has
taken honours in his class, he will not be perturbed by the superiority of others in their
various departments, because he knows that his
turn will come.

So in horticulture, while we extend our admiration to all the trees, shrubs, and flowers in our
possession, we shall derive a large gratification

and advantage from knowing everything that is
to be known—the nomenclature, the botanical
distinctions, the culture of some particular species
or family of plants.   For example, I have two or
three floral friends whose erudition is so exhaustive in their peculiar departments of knowledge
that I seem to collapse in their presence, with
sensations akin to that " sort of drop-down-dead-
ness " which a certain bishop, so Sydney Smith
informs us, desired to witness in his clergy.   If I
venture to utter, they give the plant of which
I speak some other name, or they correct my
pronunciation.   When I present my most recent
acquisition with the foolish hope that it may
surprise and please them, they call it "a dear
nice old thing, long ago superseded."   They
seem to have an intimate acquaintance with all
the nurseries and gardens of Europe, in which
their favourites are found, and they regard me
with an expression of compassionate disdain,
when I am constrained to confess that I do not
know Van Houtte.

There is, however, a limit to my depression,
and when I have reached it my spirit rises with
a swift rebound.   I am gradually leading my

tyrant within the range of a masked battery, and when I open fire I know that he will be perplexed to hide his confusion, and that he will withdraw from the battle in as genteel a form as the disagreeable surroundings will permit. We approach the Roses, of which he knows nothing, and when I ask his opinion of Nabonnand's new *Teas*, and when he replies that he has not seen them, and might manifestly have added that he had never heard of Nabonnand, I know that he is in my power; and with a suppressed but savage murmur—"Let the galled jade wince, our withers are unwrung"—I proceed, in a mean, merciless spirit of retaliation, to solicit his advice, with an anxious and deferential demeanour, on subjects which had not been previously suggested for his consideration. He tries to transfer the conversation to other topics, to pass from Polyantha to Polyanthus, but I will not let him go. I feel like the man who replied to the suggestion of a bystander that he should release his adversary whom he had knocked down in a scuffle, and would not permit to rise, "If you'd been at as much trouble as I have to get him here, you'd have a different

view of the position." Finally mercy seasons
judgment, and I take him away to luncheon in
a limp and draggled condition.

We have wandered too long from the Rock
Garden, and one always longs to return, there
is so much, and that almost, in some form or
other, throughout the year, to delight us; always
such a charming grace of congruity between the
grey stones and the flowers, as though they
were united for the mutual society, help, and
comfort which the one ought to have of the
other both in prosperity and adversity, summer
and winter, sunshine and storm. The tiny little
plants seem to nestle for warmth and cling for
protection to the stones, and the old grey stones
seem to embrace and bless them, as we grand-
fathers our children's children. What infinite
beauty in so small space! What a glow and
variety of colour!

White flowers, such as, to cite a few examples,
the Arenaria, Arabis, Anemone, Artemisia, Iberis, Silene Alpestris, and Phlox
Nelsonii.

Blue and purple, such as Aubrietia, Anemones,
Apennina and Robinsoniana, Gentians,

Campanulas, Lithospermum, Scillas, Myosotis, and Veronica.

Crimson and pink, such as Anemone fulgens,
Phlox subulata, Daphne cneorum, Silene,
and Saponaria.

Yellow, Adonis, Alyssum, Helianthemum,
dwarf Hypericum, and miniature Narcissus.

These, and treble their number, may be grown
on a small bed made from three or four cart-
loads of soil, with half a score of stones about
two feet in diameter. Thousands of small villas
in the suburbs of our towns, which have now
little more in their gardens than a few dejected
shrubs, a bed of bulbs in the Spring, and of
half-hardy plants from the nursery close by in
the summer, might thus be made ornamental
to the home, and a perpetual interest to its
inmates. I have seen this combination of stones
and flowers so tastefully arranged around the
window of a small house that the outlook was
quite picturesque, and when I accepted the invitation of the owner to "eat Alpine strawberries in Switzerland," it was difficult to believe
that some three years ago the blinds of that

window were always down to hide the ugliness
of the back yard! Almost every garden might
have its small, *multum in parvo*, collection, and
where the extent is large there should be a
separate and spacious enclosure containing beds
of various heights and proportions, and surrounded by sloping walls of irregular outline,
to exclude the view beyond; the beds should be
intersected by narrow paths made from broken
stones, and there should be steps here and there
in the higher mounds. The indentations of the
boundary walls will supply warm corners and
delectable nooks for the more tender plants.
Such an elaborate and expensive structure as
would leave room for a vigorous growth, and
would comprehend the crowd of candidates ever
increasing, and presenting irresistible charms for
admission, can only be raised at once to its completion by the possessors of abundant means, and
they are too often inclined to prefer pictures to
realities, and the "colours of the riders" to the
tints of the flower. Great results may, nevertheless, be obtained by the patient zeal of the poorer
brethren, and if I were at the commencement
instead of the close of my horticultural career,

I should lose no time in drawing my plan, and in laying down the first bed for the gradual development of my Rock Garden.

A more simple formation might be made of banks on either side of winding walks, as at Kew, but this arrangement is not nearly so attractive and picturesque as that which I have described, and would not have been preferred at Kew, where everything is done with such perfect taste, were it not impossible to establish the more elaborate system in a place of public resort. A mixed multitude of holiday folk in the narrow paths among the Alpines would be a slaughter of the innocents, whereas it may be kept in some order upon broad walks, trampling of course on every bit of vegetation which has ventured over the borders of the beds. Indeed I have known some highly educated persons who regarded this natural growth, which some of us rejoice to see, as an offensive intrusion, marring the uniformity of their box edgings and long lines of gravel, as a trespasser and vagabond, a prisoner escaping from jail to create disorder.

Alas, the Rock Garden has more cruel and potent adversaries than the rudeness of the rabble or the ignorance and indifference of the higher grades. Perpetual weeds, some of them of such respectable appearance that the gardener himself believes them to be flowers, even as pickpockets, dressed as clergymen, attend the meetings of the *élite*, and deceive the astute policeman. There are slugs and snails, gorging themselves on these dainty morsels, like the huge foul ogres of old swallowing babies as though they were oysters. Walking the other day in Piccadilly, I cast one of those furtive glances, which are not restricted to schoolboys, at the stores of Messrs. Fortnum & Mason, and as I read an announcement of " Peach-fed Hams," I thought sadly of the smaller swine browsing among my Alpine Flowers. The weeds must be uprooted, and the vermin must be destroyed by a vigilance which does not tire, although it must at times go out into the darkness to search with a lantern for its foes, and although the process of extermination is loathsome.

And so we come to the last of our Sermons in Stones. The similarity between the flowers and the weeds, the tares and the wheat, suggests a cautious investigation when we choose our com-

o

panions. There is a host of men, who claim to be gentlemen, dress, talk, look like gentlemen, who are quite devoid of the principles, the energies, and the ambitions which justify that splendid appellation. They are idle and useless: like the weeds, they cumber the ground. Not satisfied with the waste of their own time, and supposing that all their neighbours are in the state of torpid stagnation, they interfere, like the weeds, with their betters, hinder them in their work, and bore them with their vapid conversation.

At the same time, we shall do well to remember that which, in the easy and agreeable occupation of criticising others, we are so often tempted to forget—that these sermons about the mixture of the false with the true are specially intended for personal use, and that we shall be wise men if, when we have peeped over the hedge into our neighbour's garden, and have carefully counted with a scornful wonder his weeds and his failures, we shall find time to inspect our own. " A man's nature," Lord Bacon writes, " runs to herbs or weeds; therefore let them seasonably water the one, and destroy the other."

The slugs and the snails are the evil inclinations and habits, which come as the serpent in Eden, to defile and to destroy; but to all, who have the will, is given the power to overcome evil with good.

For a descriptive list of the plants most desirable for a Rock Garden, I must refer those who seek information to the catalogues of the nurserymen, who have large collections of the best varieties. There is no room for it here; and I may mention in proof that the hand-list of herbaceous plants cultivated in the Royal Gardens at Kew enumerates more than two hundred varieties of Saxifrage, and nearly one hundred of Sedum.

CHAPTER X

The Water Garden

" From north and south, from east and west,
The pride of every zone,
The fairest, rarest, and the best,
May all be made our own."

—WHITTIER's *" Hymn for the American*
Horticultural Society."

I DO not admire the appellation of a " Bog
Garden." I lost my interest in bogs, marshes,
and quagmires, when I discontinued, many years
ago, my pursuit of the jack-snipe, and even their
association with the garden fails to revive my
affection. They suggest malaria, exhalations,
unpleasant odours, Will-o'-the-wisps. As works
of art, they are too wet or too dry; they are
submerged in the rainy seasons, and they lack

moisture in the time of drought. Such was my experience in a small pond at one of the corners of my garden. I made a selection from the catalogue of a reliable purveyor, I packed my roots securely in baskets and lidless hampers, filled with congenial soil, loam and peat, and I consigned them carefully to their native element. We were subsequently favoured with the phenomenon of a hot summer. Aquarius disappeared from the signs of the Zodiac, and the Naiads departed to the English and Scotch lakes, where there is always abundance of rain, and to Ireland, where, so Fox the statesman said, "that little shower" is always going on. The baskets and hampers reappeared, and their tenantry emerged, drooping and dejected, in a green and yellow melancholy, principally yellow, until at last I dare not look them in the face, because I knew that they were being roasted alive. I am told that, under more auspicious conditions, where the soppy characteristics of the bog are more successfully maintained, the results are satisfactory; but it has not been my privilege at present to enjoy any ocular proof.

Nor do I admire, as receptacles for aquatic

plants, the tanks, or the tubs, or the basons
with the central fountains, and their dolphins,
huge-headed and curly-tailed; but where there
are pools of water, whose waters fail not, being
supplied by a running stream, then, on the
water and around it, you may have the beautiful Water Garden. Happy is the gardener
who has this gracious privilege, were it only
that he might enjoy the culture of two of
"the fairest, rarest, and the best" of all the
flowers that grow, the Flag Iris from Japan,
Iris Kæmpferi, and the Water Lilies, the *Nymphæas*, old and new.

If the water is not there, every effort should
be made to supply it by artificial means. Sometimes, though unseen, it is near. It has been
denounced as a fond thing vainly invented, but I
am quite convinced that certain persons become
sensitive, by some mysterious communication,
of the existence of water in the earth beneath
them; and it is said that when the discovery is
made, a willow wand, which is carried in the
hand, is visibly agitated. Mr. Ingram, the late
head-gardener at Belvoir Castle, showed me the
spot where a man, who then lived in the neigh-

bouring village of Denton, had suddenly stopped, and declared that there was water not far below. It was speedily found, and I saw it flowing down the slopes, and in the pool below the *Aponogeton distachyon*, with an abundance of its fair and fragrant flowers.

Of all the plants which must be grown in contiguity with water, either on its banks or where it may be introduced whenever it is required, *Iris Lævigata* (syn. *Kæmpferi*) is the most beautiful. Our most grandiloquent adjectives, our *sesquipedalia verba*, are so enfeebled, as I have shown, by their perpetual application to insignificant objects, that they are altogether impotent. I shall not attempt to describe it, beyond a few simple details, but I shall never forget my first introduction to a large bed in full flower, outside the end of the lake at Newstead Abbey, where the water could be admitted at will into the sluices between the rows of the Iris. The varieties selected in, and sent direct from, Japan, were somewhat like the Clematis in form, and were six to eight inches in diameter, and were of diverse colours—white, rose, blue, purple, grey, and crimson. They evoked a

delicious surprise and excitement, very rarely
enjoyed by one who has lived his life among
the flowers, and has seen the most famous
gardens of England, Scotland, France, and Italy,
including *La Mortola*, which is to me the most
charming of them all. It was one of those
happy astonishments, which "when they seldom
come, they wished for come"; and though the
attraction was some distance from the house, I
was perpetually wandering to and fro, under
an irresistible fascination, to this iris and apple
of mine eye.

It is possible, we are told, to grow this eximi-
ous flower away from the vicinity of streams
and pools, in soils naturally moist or artificially
watered, and I have an interesting and instructive letter from my friend, and the friend of
all gardeners, Mr. Peter Barr, on this subject.
"*Iris Kæmpferi,*" he writes, "will often thrive
on ground which one would not choose for it,
and will fail on ground which one would have
supposed to be most congenial. At one time
I bestowed a great amount of trouble upon
them, but was not so successful as when I gave
them a less anxious care. One thing is that

they should have a moist, hot place in summer, and a fairly dry place in winter—a combination difficult to realise in this climate. They who have seen them growing in Japan inform us that the soil in which they grow is a sort of quagmire. Our *Iris Kæmpferi* was in the driest part of the Tooting grounds this year (1889), and the quantity of buds surpassed anything that I have seen, but the flowers were comparatively small. On one occasion I tried, as an experiment, a bed made of loam and peat, one part being exposed to the sun and the other in the shade: the former had plants three or four feet in height, the latter were less and the flowers few.

"I would recommend you to get some sleepers from the railway station, and to place them on bricks to secure drainage; to fill them up with a suitable compost to within three inches of the surface, planting the Iris a foot or eighteen inches apart each way, the collar of the plant being level with the surface of the soil, which must be kept open so as to catch all the sun's rays in spring and summer, and must be protected against severe frosts by bracken or other fronds in the winter. In May they must have water, and if the weather is dry, two good soakings in the week, with a slight admixture of mild manure, until they have ceased to flower."

I conclude, nevertheless, from all that I have seen, heard, and read on this subject, that you cannot realise *Iris Kæmpferi* in its marvellous perfection unless you have at your command a constant supply of water during the season of its growth and efflorescence; and such an arrangement, made by pipes and taps, as at Newstead from the lake hard by, is preferable to planting on the banks. This will not be required when the flowers fade, and the plant will take care of itself, rest, and be thankful.

Where there is peat, the *Rhododendron* should be reflected in the water. Some of the *Spiræas* grow luxuriantly; and there should be *Rushes*, *Reeds*, and *Eulalias*, with trees, the *Weeping Willow*, the *Weeping Cypress*, the *Laburnum*, the *Hippophæ Ramnoides* (Sea Buckthorn), a very ornamental shrub, in spite of its harsh designation, as it may be seen growing by the water at Kew, with its bright berries visible from afar. All these,

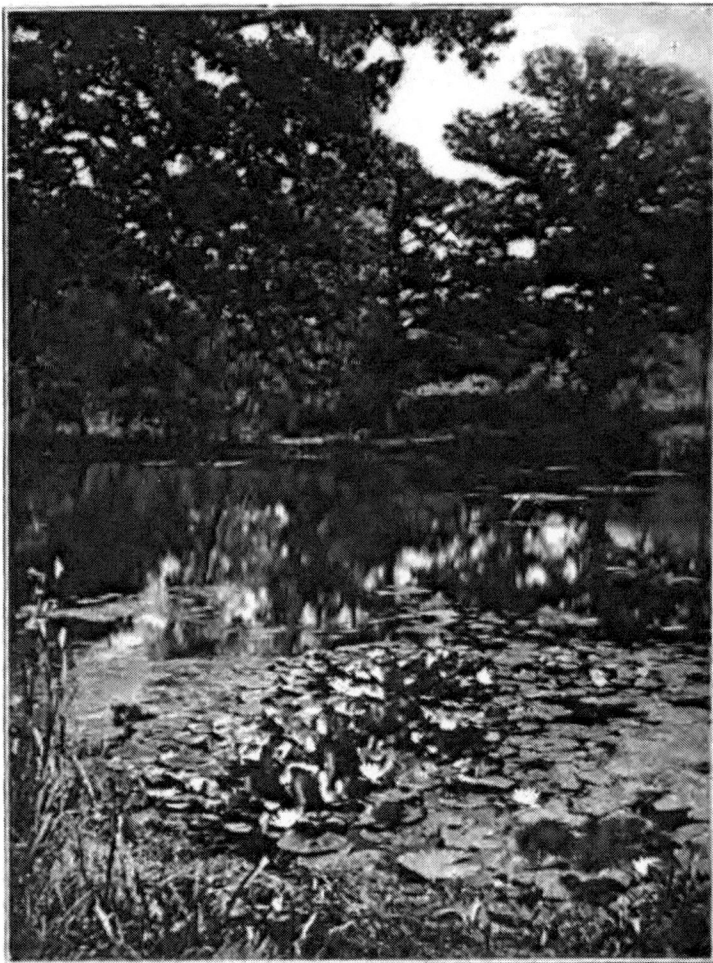

THE WATER GARDEN

grown singly or in groups, must be planted at intervals, and must not crowd the banks.

When the *Water Lilies* (the *Nymphæas*) introduced into this country by Monsieur Latour-Marliac from France are acclimatised and proved to be hardy, as there is every reason to hope, they will undoubtedly maintain their supremacy, like those lovely Nymphs, the Naiads, over the lake and the pool, and in alliance with their elder sisterhood, the white *Nymphæa* and the yellow *Nuphar*, will reign in all the power and glory with which Britannia rules the seas. There is still some doubt as to this consummation; and the pessimists, and they who can hardly realise such an unexpected joy, are alarmed to hear of tubs, which may be removed, and tanks, which may be protected in the water, and even of heating apparatus underneath the waters, suggesting the application of hot-water bottles to the chilly toes of the Nymphs; but we may be sure that if the present specimens should be found unable to resist the severities of our climate, the science which discovered the possibility will persevere, until by intermarriage and experience in culture such a vigorous con-

stitution is attained as shall insure its perpetuity;
the true gardener's motto is *nil desperandum*, and
when he has once seen the Marliac lilies he
will not let them go; but from the accounts
which we received from America, and from our
own leading nurserymen, one of whom affirms
that "they are as hardy and as easy to grow
as the common lilies of our English ponds,"
there seems to be small fear of difficulty, much
less of despair.

Meanwhile

> " It stirs the blood in an old man's heart,
> And it makes his pulses fly."

only to read of

Nymphæa Ellisiana (free habit, flowers of a
brilliant carmine rose colour, very sweet
scented),

N. Fulva (flowers large, light yellow, tinted
with rose),

N. Gloriosa (large, ample, bold foliage. Blossoms fragrant, very large indeed, of a
deep brilliant rose or rose purple),

N. Laydekeri Liliacea (deep rosy crimson, and
then golden yellow),

N. Marliacea Flammea (blossoms very large—
   bright carmine rose),

N. Robinsoni (large reddish vermilion flowers),

N. Sanguinea (flowers of intense blood purple,
   tea-rose scented),

N. Seignouretii (flowers deep orange, shaded
   with golden yellow towards the base);

but the reader who, having the aquatic accommodation, may desire to introduce these allurements,
must be warned, before giving a large order, that
they are expensive luxuries, varying in cost from
four to ten guineas each. There are much less
costly varieties, such as *Marliaceas Albida, Carnea,
Chromatella, Odorata, Exquisita, Gigantea*, and *Sul-
phurea*, which may be bought for half-a-guinea
apiece.

These Lilies have in certain localities cruel foes
both in and over the water, like that unhappy
flying fish whom the dolphin pursues below,
and the albatross attacks above the surface.
The rats—" there be land rats and water rats "—
will nibble the roots, and the swans and wild-
fowl will sometimes peck at the flowers.

There are many other attractive plants for
the waterside and the water. For the banks

and shallows, the Sweet Flag (*Acorus*), the Water
Plantain (*Alisma,*) the Flowering Rush (*Butomus*),
the Bulrush (*Scirpus*), the Bog Arum (*Calla*), the
Marsh Marigold (*Caltha*), the Prickly Rhubarb
(*Gunnera*), the Purple Loosestrife (*Lythrum*),
the Royal (*Osmunda*), and other Ferns, the
Meadow Sweet (*Spiræa*), the Golden Club
(*Orontium*), the Buck Bean (*Menyanthes*). To
be submerged, the Water Hawthorn (*Aponogeton*),
all the Water Lilies (*Nymphæa*), the Pickerel
Weed (*Pontederia*), the Arrowhead (*Sagittaria*),
the Dwarf Water Lily (*Villarsia Nymphæides*).
These have their special claims, and should be
included whenever there is accommodation, but
where the extent of water is small for aquatic
and semi-aquatic plants, I would urge its occupation by the *Nymphæas* of Latour-Marliac, and
the *Iris Lævigata* of Kæmpfer.

CHAPTER XI

The Wild Garden

" A Garden wild, but not without a plan." •
—Pope.

LEAVING the Naiads for the Dryads (when
the Eton boy was asked the difference between them, he gave it as his opinion that
the Naiads were Wet Bobs, and the Dryads
Dry), we will pass quickly through the Pinetum
and Fernery, included in our Ideal Garden,
because I have no information to give about
them which deserves the reader's attention. I
am in possession of two gardens, but one is on
the clay and the other on the chalk, neither
of them being congenial for the growth of

coniferous trees, and I have to restrict my admiration to a few of the hardier varieties of the Cedar, the Cypress, and the Pine, having learned from a sorrowful experience that the more tender varieties deteriorate and die. As to Ferns, although a great admirer, and a witness of their successful culture by my wife, I am profoundly ignorant, and invariably quicken my pace when I come with visitors into proximity. There is so much obtrusive curiosity to know the difference between a *Lycopodium* and a *Seliginella*, whether *Polypodium* or *Polystychum* has the larger share of your affection, and which is your favourite *Gymnostachium*. It is a dreadful temptation to feign deafness, to run a red herring across the line, and to say "That's a fine *Hart's Tongue*, is it not?" (everybody knows *Hart's Tongue*), and so it is best to hurry onwards, having the further inducement that if you reply, "I don't know," they will think that you mean "I won't tell."

A Wild Garden, in which those who had extensive grounds, and loved the beautiful, sought either to form an arboretum, a plantation of trees and shrubs in formal arrangement, or to intro-

duce evergreens and flowers among the woods
which they found in existence, has long been a
great enjoyment to those few in number who
have had the energy to accomplish that which
their zeal designed. It sounds like a misnomer,
but "the Wilderness" of our ancestors was as
methodical and artificial as a canal or a palisade.
We are told by contemporary writers that a
hundred and fifty years ago the usual method
of contriving Wildernesses was to divide the
whole compass of the ground either into squares
and angles, just as New York is divided now, or
into circles and other figures, making the walks
correspondent to them, planting by the side of
these walks, hedges of Lime, Elm, Hornbeam,
&c., and filling the quarters within with various
kinds of trees. Even the most enlightened gardeners of those days, although they expressed
their dislike of these compositions as being "too
trim and too trite," and their disapproval of the
hedges, which grew so high that the pedestrian
saw nothing of the trees beyond, proposed
open spaces for obelisks and statues, domes and
banquet-halls; that the trees should rise one
above another to the tallest in the centre of

P

the quarter, and, so far as it was possible, should have the same uniform height in their different gradations as they sloped down to the walks.

There were indications of a higher appreciation and a purer taste, where it is recorded that, near the walks and openings, *Roses, Honeysuckles, Spiræas,* and other kinds of low-flowering shrubs, which might be always kept dwarf, were planted closely together, and below them, *Primroses, Violets, Daffodils,* and many other sorts of wood-flowers—not in a straight line, but rather to appear accidental, as in a natural wood. Behind the first row of shrubs were planted *Syringas, Cytisus, Althæa frutex, Mezereon,* and other flowering shrubs of a middle growth; and beyond these *Laburnums, Lilacs, Guelder Roses,* and others of a larger growth.

Evergreens were arranged on the same graduated scale. In the first line, next to the walks, the *Laurus tinus,* the *Box,* the *Spurge Laurel,* the *Juniper,* the *Savin,* and other dwarfs; behind these, *Laurels, Hollies, Arbutus.* In the third line, *Alaternus* (*Rhamnus* or *Buckthorn*), *Phillyreas, Yew, Cypress, Virginia, Cedar;* and behind these the *Evergreen Firs* and *Pines.*

Evergreen and deciduous trees were to be kept
as strictly apart as the men and the women in
some of our churches, according, as it is said, to
ancient custom; and the Rev. Mr. Hanbury, in
an elaborate work on Gardening, in writing on
this subject finds "tongues in trees," and suggesting a plantation of deciduous trees on the
one side of a lawn, and of evergreen trees on
the other, he takes up his parable and gives us
a striking object-lesson, a sermon greatly to be
admired for its brevity. These plantations, he
writes, in the winter months will afford an agreeable contrast, on the one side presenting to the
view, during that dreary season, the deciduous
trees, divested of their honours, emblems of our
approaching fate, whilst on the other side the
eye is relieved by the prospect of the evergreens flourishing as in a perpetual spring, emblems of immortality. Dreary indeed would be
our shrubberies, borders, and beds, *luci a non
lucendo*, without our *Aucubas, Arbutus, Hollies*,
and *Laurus tinus*, although I so far agree with
the injunction that in the Wild Garden and
woods the evergreens should not be planted
singly but in groups. It is very refreshing to

come suddenly on a clump of *Laurels, Hollies,* or *Berberis.* In days long ago, when I walked with my gun among the grand old oaks of the Shire Wood, now known as Sherwood Forest, I remember a spot where we suddenly emerged from the yellow bracken and deciduous trees in front of a large clump of glossy evergreens, and the same direction was always given by the head-keeper —"Now, my lords and gentlemen, if you please, all in a breast through the Rosydendrums." That was the period of life in which I realised Lord Byron's words, not far from his home, but very far from his intention,

"There is a pleasure in the pathless woods,"

entering bravely with the beaters into the roughest thicket, and coming out on "the Ride," where the guns were posted, with cheek bleeding and jacket torn, but with a great jubilation of heart, when my attendant keeper had the woodcock in his hand! As time goes on we leave the briars for the "nick," wherein some facilities of passage have been made by the bill-hook, passing thence to the main avenues; and when duty demands or age disables, taking our final departure from the woods; but enjoying the Garden, and its supplement the Wild Garden, so long as life shall last, finding therein rest and renewal, while we have the power to work, and when that fails, in sunny corners, protected from the cold, or in pleasant arbours, screened from the heat, the peace which passes understanding in its full assurance of hope.

As with the Garden, so with the Wild Garden, it is impossible to give definite designs or absolute decrees, where the extent is unknown, the site and its surroundings so different. In my suggestion of " an Ideal Garden," my design was to help those who were making a new garden, whether on a large or a lesser scale—for the dimensions might be easily reduced—to work upon that which is called the Natural system; to remember that *ars est celare artem*, to avoid straight lines and angles, substituting easy and graceful curves; and it is possible, of course, for those who assent to this principle, but whose gardens are not in conformity, to make such alterations as may promote their views. In treating of the Wild Garden, it will, I think, be the most successful scheme to adopt a theory of development and to make such gradual additions to our small beginning as may be convenient.

Such was the process which had been pursued in the first Wild Garden which I was privileged to see under the auspices of the proprietor, the Hon. and Rev. Mr. Boscawen, a most genial and enthusiastic gardener, at his Rectory in Cornwall. In a long plantation adjoining his garden, he selected a spot not far from the entrance, in which he thought that a group of flowers would be effective, and having cleared the ground, which was open to the sun, and not under the shadow or drip of the trees, from rank grass and weeds, he brought in a quantity of good soil, and planted the bed. Every year he multiplied his stores, until he had a long series of sweet surprises for his friends. I do not remember the varieties which he chose — the memories of the man, who, like the butterfly, is "roving for ever from flower to flower," become inextricably mixed—but the general effect was delightful. The flowers looked so fresh and bright, as though they rejoiced in their emancipation from the formal parterre, and were blithe as birds just escaped from an aviary.

Mr. Boscawen was an expert, and knew what, where, and how to plant; and he who would succeed in his Wild Garden must study the properties of his soil, the habits of his plants, and their mutual adaptation.   In this, as in every other cultural enterprise, we must be true to our first great principle; and when we seek in all humility to copy Nature, we shall always find signs and indications to inform and guide us.   We may surely infer that where we have the wild flowers of indigenous growth, there with due attention we may produce their congeners; that where we have the wood *Anemones*, white and blue, we might have them purple and scarlet; and so where we find the *Bluebell* or *Wood Hyacinth*, the *Clematis*, *Crane's bill*, *Cowslip*, *Crocus*, *Cyclamen*, *Daffodil*, *Forget-me-not*, *Foxglove*, *Honeysuckle*, *Iris*, *Lily*, *Meadow-sweet*, *Orchis*, *Primrose*, *Rose*, *Thyme*, *Viola*, we may introduce their illustrious synonyms and descendants with confident hopes of success.   We must remember at the same time to make careful preparations to receive them, providing the diet and supplying the service to which they have been accustomed, or they will be unable to assimilate the coarser food,

and will resent our negligence by reverting to
type.   You could not remove the son of a
"self-made" millionaire from his luxurious
home to the cottage of his grandfather, and limit
his *menu* to bread and cheese, cow's liver and
cold bacon, pig's fry and buttermilk, without
serious peril to his health.

Before the addition of novelties I should
endeavour, in the formation of a Wild Garden,
to obtain an abundant supply of the wild flowers
themselves, and so far from civilising the natives
from off the face of the earth, or imitating the
Pilgrim Fathers, who, when they landed, fell
on their knees, and then proceeded to fall on
the aborigines, I should make every effort to
encourage and increase them.   Not many sights
are fairer to the eye, not many odours are sweeter
to the nose, than those which are given to us
from the Primrose bank; no Persian woof—

"Persicos odi, puer, apparatus "—

to compare with Nature's carpet of *Anemone*, *Bluebell*, *Cyclamen*, *Cowslip*, *Daffodil*, and *Forget-me-
not*.   How beautiful the *Foxgloves* rising out
of the *Ferns!*   The *Traveller's Joy*, the *Honey-*

suckle, the *Rose*, on the boundary fences without, and elsewhere within!

Having these wild flowers in plenteous store, I should import an appropriate selection from their good-looking relations; *e.g.* the *Cowslip* would suggest the *Oxlip* and *Polyanthus*; the *Daffodil*, a group of *Horsfieldii*; *Traveller's Joy*, *Montana* and other *Clematis*; the *Forget-me-not*, *Myosotis dissitiflora*; the *Meadow-sweet*, an assortment of *Spiræas*; the *Orchis* of *Cypripedium*, *Spectabile*, and other hardy varieties; the *Primrose* of modern *Primulas*; and the *Rosa Canina* of the *Ayrshire*, *Sempervirens*, and other climbing Roses, of the Japanese *Rugosa*, the *China*, the *Monthly*, and the *Sweet Briar*.

And then I should go, and I advise my readers to go, to the supreme authorities; to Mr. William Robinson, who in his "Wild Garden" (inscribed to his proud friend, the Dean of Rochester) revived the idea of a supplemental garden, and taught that idea how to shoot from hedges and ditches, walls and ruins, lanes and copses, shrubberies, plantations and woods; and to Miss Jekyll, who in her "Wood and Garden" has given to horticultural literature the most perfect example of practical wisdom in combination with poetical thought. We know now the secret and the source of her artistic design and manual adroitness; they spring from a quick perception and a devout admiration of "whatsoever things are lovely." It is her reverent appreciation of beauty, which empowers her first to realise for herself, and then to impart to her readers, a sense of the grace and of the glory which surround us, and which constrain us to join in the hymn of praise, "Oh all ye green things upon the earth, bless ye the Lord; praise Him and magnify Him for ever." It is this divine affection which paints for us pictures far more excellent than the photographs of her camera, though these too are excellent, as when she writes of January :—

"The ground was a warm carpet of pale rusty fern; tree stem, and branch, and twig show tender colour harmonies of grey bark and silver-grey lichen, only varied by the feathery masses of birch spray. Now the splendid richness of the common holly is more than ever impressive, with its solid masses of full deep colour, and its wholesome look of perfect health and vigour."

Again, when referring to the beautiful form of the deciduous trees divested of their foliage :—

" It is only in winter, when they are bare of leaves, that we
can fully enjoy their splendid structure and design, their admirable qualities of duly apportioned strength and grace of poise,
and the way in which the spread of the many-branched head
has its equivalent in the wide-reaching ground-grasp of the
roots."

And of the fragrance from the trees :—

"There are balmy days in mid-April when the whole garden
is fragrant with sweet-briar.   Passing upward through the copse
the warm air draws an odour almost as sweet, but infinitely more
subtle, from the fresh green of the young birches.   Higher still
the fresh leafage of the larch gives a delightful perfume ; *and
it seems as though* it were the office of these mountain trees,
already nearest the high heaven, to offer for their new life an
incense of praise."

Alas, of how many it must be said, "Eyes have
they, and see not; noses have they, and smell
not."

One more short extract :—

"June is here—thank God for lovely June !   The soft
cooing of the wood-dove, the glad song of many birds, the
flitting of butterflies, the hum of all the little winged people
among the branches, the sweet earth scents all seem to say
the same, with endless reiteration, never wearying because so
gladsome."

Long reign this Queen of Spades, as long, as
happily, as Victoria, Queen of Hearts!

We shall find in Mr. Robinson's book long

lists of the best plants suitable for naturalisation
in poor soil, of vigorous habit for the Wild
Garden, of fine foliage and graceful form, of
trailers and climbers, of varieties which love
moisture, peat, chalk, and sand; and Miss
Jekyll will warn us that whatever may be our
soil or our site, the attempt to improve Nature,
even in her rudest dress, is a very perilous
process, and that there is need of the most
anxious caution lest we disfigure that we would
adorn. He who proposes to lay out a Wild
Garden must have very distinctly in his mind's
eye the effect which he intends to produce; and
when, as it occasionally happens, he has no eye
either in his mind or in his head, the results
are ghastly. "Unthinking persons," Miss Jekyll
writes, "rush to the conclusion that they can
put any garden plants into any wild places, and
that that is wild gardening. I have seen woody
places, that were already perfect with their own
simple charm, just muddled and spoilt by a
reckless planting of garden refuse, and healthy
hillsides, already sufficiently and beautifully
clothed with native vegetation, made to look
lamentably silly by the planting of a nursery-

man's mixed lot of exotic conifers. In my own case, I have always devoted the most careful consideration to any bit of wild gardening I thought of doing, never allowing myself to decide upon it till I felt thoroughly assured that the place seemed to ask for the planting in contemplation, and that it would be distinctly a gain in pictorial value."

Even the rabbits sometimes forbid the madness of the planter by devouring his exotics in their early growth; and I therefore venture in the conclusion of my chapter to repeat my advice, that *Wild Flowers and their near relations should be the principal tenants of the Wild Garden.*

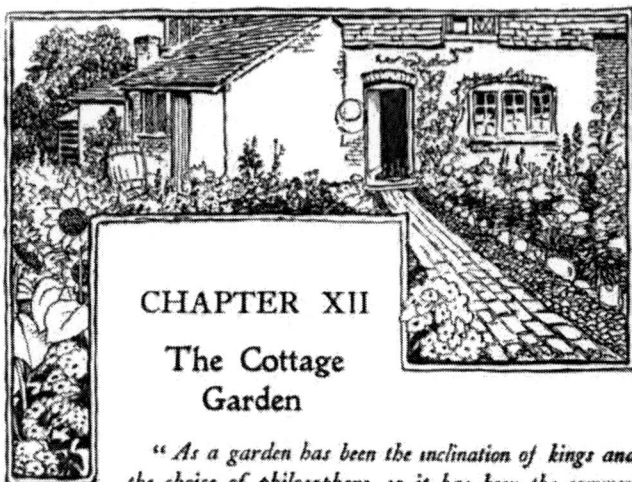

CHAPTER XII

The Cottage Garden

"As a garden has been the inclination of kings and the choice of philosophers, so it has been the common favourite of public and private men, a pleasure of the greatest, and the care of the meanest, and, indeed, an employment and possession for which none is too high or low."—SIR WILLIAM TEMPLE.

"In the culture of flowers there cannot, by their very nature, be anything solitary or exclusive. The wind that blows over the cottage porch sweeps over the grounds of the nobleman, and as the rain descends on the just and on the unjust, so it communicates to all gardens, both rich and poor, an interchange of pleasure and enjoyment."—CHARLES DICKENS.

I WENT to Paris in my *première jeunesse*, to improve my knowledge and pronunciation of the French language, and when I had spent a month at the Hotel Meurice, where we all spoke English, including the waiters, I came home, and might have been appropriately labelled as a "returned empty." I enjoyed none the less when I reached our shores my transfer from the lumbering *diligence*, crawling over the dreary plain which lies betwixt Paris and the sea, with the incessant cracking of the whip, and the monotonous tinkling of the bells, to the box seat of the Dover Mail, and sat behind four well-bred, well-fed, well-groomed horses, trotting cheerily their ten miles an hour, over the hills and through the valleys, by the woods and the copses, the cornfields and pastures, the orchards and the hop-yards, of the land, which, go where we will, is ever the glory of all lands to our English eyes and hearts.

Especially I was delighted with the wayside cottages and their bright little gardens, although I had lived among them all my life, and had only left them a few weeks before. There were the Lilacs and Laburnums, the Gilliflowers, the Sweet Williams, and the Cloves, the Bachelor's Buttons and the Love-lies-bleeding, the Larkspur and the Lupin, the Monthly, the Cabbage, the old White Damask, the York and Lancaster, the Moss, and the Sweet Briar Rose. The bees were working in and out of their hives, like busy men in the City, and the butterflies were flirting among the flowers, like idle men in the Park. The canary, brought out into the sunshine, was singing from his cage of wire, or the magpie was chattering from his cage of wicker.

A pretty picture, which artists love to paint; but we want something more. A ruin is picturesque, and as an accession to a pic-nic quite charming, but when it is contemplated as a residence or as a source of income, the most zealous antiquarian must allow that it leaves much to be desired. Every labourer should not only have this bit of brightness about a home, which looks so bare and cold without it, and should be taught to appreciate and to maintain its beauty, but to combine also that which is good for food with that which is pleasant to the eye, the kindly fruits of the earth in due season. He should have apple-tree, plum-tree, and cherry-tree, his bushes of gooseberries and currants, his potatoes and greens, in addition to his garden of flowers. He should refresh his mind with the ornamental, and his body with the useful, not imitating the rigid economy of one of our Nottinghamshire squires who, being asked why he no longer kept deer in his park, replied, "They clip no wool."

They who earnestly desire to promote the happiness of their fellow-men should bring all their influence to bear upon *the home*, to increase the attachments, which endear a man to his home. Nowhere else will he find this happiness if he does not find it there; and therefore those adjuncts should be applied and those interests should be educed, which suggest the pleasant and profitable occupation of leisure hours, and so produce content.

"The pleasantest work of human industry," Cowley writes in a letter to Evelyn, "is the improvement of something, which we can call our own," and he who shall persuade and help the cottager to put this axiom to the test, and to realise the power which he possesses to improve his surroundings, will deserve not only the gratitude of the individual man, but of the community at large. He will have transformed a drone into a bee, and he will have done more to keep his brother from drunkenness than all the pamphlets that ever were printed, and all the

blue ribbons that ever were flaunted over proud
Pharisaic hearts. He will have added not only
to our respectability, but to our food supply.
No one can attend the exhibitions of our Cottage
Gardening Societies, without knowing that some
of these labourers are, so far as their means go,
first-class gardeners. I remember a remark of
Archbishop Benson's, " When the working man
knows *the reason why*—why he should belong
to the Church of his fathers—there is no more
zealous Churchman ; " and so it may be said that
when the working man discovers the delights of
horticulture, he becomes an artist. I have seen in
both cases many conspicuous proofs—working men
coming by scores to church on the last morning
of a Mission, before daybreak, when I had to feel
my way along the wall for the vestry door ; and
working men exhibiting flowers and vegetables,
roses especially, as at Nottingham, in excellent
condition. But these examples are few and the
.process slow, and blessed is he who shall increase
or expedite.

For these reasons we must regard with a most
thankful and respectful sympathy, and with all
the practical support which we can offer, the endea-

vours made by our County Councils to advise and assist cottage gardeners. The arrangements for this county of Kent are admirable. The Technical Education Committee have appointed as their "Horticultural Instructor," Mr. Wright, F.R.H.S., whom I have known for many years as an accomplished expert and an able writer, to give lectures, intelligible to all, at certain centres on the culture of flowers, fruit, and vegetables, illustrated by diagrams and lantern slides; personally to inspect the gardens and allotments, to superintend the award of prizes for the best culture, the best collections of flowers, vegetables, and fruits; and to establish School Gardens in different parts of the country, providing the boys with tools, seeds, &c. These pupils in due course become holders of full-sized allotments, with all the advantages of their training to help them in their work.

Mr. Wright has written some concise but comprehensive manuals on the subject of Cottage Gardens and allotments, such as "The Horticultural Primer," "Garden Flowers and Plants," and has edited a most reliable treatise on "Vegetable Culture," by Mr. Alexander Dean.

The Council have shown in many other ways their anxious interest and thoughtful insight with regard to the welfare of their fellow-men, instructing them as to the keeping of bees, the rearing of poultry, the preservation of their fruit; and because they know the calamitous atrocities which are daily wrought by ignorance in the preparation of food through the length and breadth of the land, they not only teach the husband how to grow his vegetables, but they show his wife how to cook them. In the last year 515 meetings, held at 14 centres, have been attended by 12,861 pupils.

These laudable endeavours to increase the comforts of the farm-labourer and the artisan by providing pleasant and profitable occupation for his leisure hours, better gardens for the cottagers in the village, and more numerous allotments for the mechanics in the town, have been made in so many other counties, that even they who were adverse to the new form of authority, are almost persuaded that in a multitude of Councillors there is wisdom. The Technical Education Committee of the County Council of Surrey, recognising the fact that

Horticulture is the oldest of the Arts, and the foundation of all others, is especially anxious, and has made arrangements accordingly, not only for gardens in which boys may be taught while they are at school, but for "Continuation Gardens," in which they may receive further instruction, when they have left it.   We all know the temptations which beset us at this period of our lives, to discontinue lessons and to forget that which we have learnt.   At the instigation and by the help of the Council, schoolmasters have qualified themselves to teach the principles and practice of horticulture both to their old pupils and to the cottagers around. The report gives a striking proof of the value of this continuous education.   It is stated that in France there are 28,000 schools with gardens attached to them, and it is now made imperative that masters of elementary schools in the rural districts must be capable of giving practical instruction in the cultivation of the soil; but this instruction is only given to children, and not to youths, and when Mons. Henri de Vilmorin, the most famous of the French horticulturists, was informed of this continuation system, he expressed his great admiration and his anxious desire that it should be adopted in France, which as yet had no such advantage.

When these pupils come to manhood, it should be made as easy as the surroundings permit for the industrious exercise of their skill. The landlord will find in them the best of tenants. In the *Nineteenth Century* for March 1899, Lord Carrington confidently asserts that "allotments and small holdings are not only a benefit to the agricultural labourers, but a direct advantage to the landlords themselves." He demonstrates the fact from his own experience. He has 1400 tenants in the environs of High Wycombe, who cultivate from one tenth of an acre to an acre each. The rent varies from 20s. to 50s. per acre, and many acres yield £30 worth of produce, with all expenses paid. On his landed estates in Buckinghamshire and Wiltshire his lordship has 1000 village allotments let at from 8s. to 30s. per acre. Not one of these tenants is in arrear of rent, and the land is better cultivated, cleaner, and more productive. In the year 1881 he had in one parish 23 tenants, occupying 11 farms and 12 small holdings; he has

now 105 tenants, of whom 70 have allotments,
26 have small holdings of from 4 to 40 acres,
and 9 have farms of 70 acres and upwards.
Another proof that these allotments pay, is given
by the applications made to the Holland County
Council in South Lincolnshire.   Prior to 1887,
in the 19 parishes of the South Holland District
there were only 130 acres under allotment cultivation : now there are 2000.

I would earnestly appeal to all who have
influence to support these efforts of the County
Councils, and the great landed proprietors, and
to do this from the highest motive, from our
love as Christians, and from our duty as patriots,
to bear one another's burden, and to work for
the common weal.   To me it seems that it is
not a charitable concession, nor a matter of
expediency, but an obligation, a right, and a
claim, that the labourer should have some share
in the land.   "He that ploweth should plow in
hope, and he that thresheth in hope should be
partaker of his hope.   The husbandman *that
laboureth* must be first partaker of the fruits."

Squires and parish priests (and I have had experience in both these vocations, and know what

each may do) can be most powerful allies in this noble enterprise, this happy endeavour to convince their neighbours that, be it never so humble, there's no place like home. The former may grant small additions of land, and may advise the tenant how to make the best of it. He may give bricks for a sty, and timber for a hovel, should prosperity suggest a cow. He may request his head-gardener and his farm-bailiff to pay an occasional visit, and the former might spare a few roots from his herbaceous border, a shrub or a tree from his "nursery." These extensions and kindnesses should be the rewards of industry, and, encouraging the recipient, would promote it in others. It is sad to hear the complaint from labourers, that although the private soldier may rise to command a regiment, the shop-boy become a wealthy tradesman, the railway porter master of a station, he who works on the farm has no hope of more ample means—only a dismal prevision of lumbago and parish pay. Hence the exodus to the factories and to the mines.

Clergymen may co-operate by their sympathy, their commendations of successful culture, and their intercessions with those who can give material help. If they are gardeners (as they ought to be, if only for their own recreation and nutriment), they can give advice, lend books and garden newspapers. I have lived to see good results from a custom which I observed, some fifty years ago, of taking the boys of my Sunday-school for walks by the brook and in the fields to gather wild flowers in the summer-tide, and to arrange them in posies. I took with me the small volumes by Ann Pratt, with coloured illustrations, and from these we learned the names and habits, with other information, of the specimens which we collected. In the interval between that time and this, I have been much gratified to meet with those who associate the love of flowers, which has never left them, with our Sunday evening walks. In cities and towns, far from the meadow and the wood, they have cherished in small gardens, window-sills, and flower-pots, the old affection. Not long ago, after responding to a toast at a City banquet, with some allusion to this floral fidelity, I noticed as I sat down that the toast-master, a stately and august personage, with much dignity of demeanour and power of voice, silently placed a little card on the table before me, on which was written, "As a boy I captured first prize for wild flowers in my native county, Devon." In a moment my thoughts sped away from the brilliant lights, the gay costumes, the exotics, and the strife of tongues, to the merry faces of the lads with the campion and the meadow-sweet, and the honeysuckles and the roses, in their hands.

"First prize for wild flowers." The parson may help in the formation and management of the Cottage-Gardeners' Show, but I would say to him, *experto crede*, and be cautious. Where, as in the counties of Kent and Surrey, the County Councils undertake to award prizes, on a regulated scale, and after the inspection of their own officers, to cultural success, you may rest assured that nothing better could be done, and that by accepting this superior knowledge instead of trusting your own inexperience in the construction of a new society, you will escape many risks of disappointment, and they whom you design to benefit many temptations to deception, dishonesty, envy, hatred, malice, and all uncharitableness.

I would recommend, nevertheless, a summer exhibition, with prizes of a small amount, in the village schoolroom, of wild flowers and window plants, for the children and mothers of the poor. When there is no garden, these window plants are greatly valued, both in the country and in the towns. There are thousands of Tim Linkinwaters, who think it worth a run upstairs to smell their mignonette, or a descent to the back yard to contemplate their double wallflower; and there's many a sickly, bedridden, humpbacked boy, who, when the weather is fine, crawls out of bed and draws a chair close to the window to look at his hyacinths grown in a cracked jug. Miss Jekyll relates in "Wood and Garden" how a factory lad in one of the great Northern manufacturing towns advertised in a mechanical paper that he wanted a tiny garden in a window-box— would somebody help him? Somebody (I have my conjectures) sent him a box, three feet by ten inches, with little plants of mossy and silvery saxifrage and a few small bulbs. Even some stones were sent, for it was to be a rock garden with two hills and a long valley. "Somebody" seems to have known somehow of the boy's delight, when the pure white of the snowdrop and the brilliant blue of the squill came forth in his attic window under that grey, soot-laden sky, and it was his glad surprise

> " To watch the matchless working of a power
> Which shuts within its seed the future flower."

In the country, the window garden of the cottager is generally filled with geraniums, fuchsias, musk, balsams, &c., so highly esteemed that they are often permitted to monopolise the light, and so carefully tended, watered, and washed, that their growth and efflorescence are remarkable

CHAPTER XIII

The Children's Garden

" And little footsteps lightly print the ground."—GRAY.

I WOULD begin the education of a gardener even before he came to the School Garden, and would encourage from the first one of the earliest spontaneous instincts, which are apparent in the family of the grand old gardener and his wife; in the children of the Queen, who had their little gardens at Osborne; of the labourer, grubbing by the wayside hedge or in the gorse of the common; and of the mechanic, amid the rank growth of the railway embankment.

When a mother asked a philosopher at what age she should commence the education of her child, he replied, having ascertained that the boy had seen six summers, "Madam, you have lost five years." Hence the value of the *Kinder Garten* to note and develop all the inclinations which are good, to repress those that are evil, and to teach discrimination between flowers and weeds. You cannot begin too soon. He who exchanges the rocking-horse for a donkey, the donkey for a pony, the pony for a cob, and the cob for a hunter, shall

" Witch the world with noble horsemanship."

In Naturâ non datur saltus, the progress is gradual, not by leaps and bounds; there are no "Lifts" from ignoranee to knowledge, from the base to the heights of Parnassus. There is no cramming in a true education.

The best of all lessons is an object-lesson; so thought St. Patrick, when he taught with the trefoil in his hand. The ear, as Horace assures us, is a slow "coach," when compared with the eye, as a pupil teacher. Children in a garden, a combination of the most charming things in the world, are learning unconsciously to admire beauty, and to recognise the first condition of success in their obedience to the immutable law of *Work*.

The external results may not be propitious. In the Deanery Garden, the soil cultivated by our grandchildren has only produced at present a few large scollop shells, a biscuit tin, and four bricks, but I am quite satisfied with the invisible. Friends remonstrate, "How can you let them make such a mess?" My reply is, "They are making *mind*, refinement, not only for themselves, but for others. When they come to manhood and womanhood, they will make the world a little brighter with things pleasant to the eye and good for food. Best of all, they are learning the rudiments of religion—to appreciate whatsoever things are lovely, whatsoever things are pure, and so to draw nearer to Him, who taught and teaches still from the common objects around us, and commands us to "consider the lilies."

Failures and absurdities are of course abundant in the beginning of our experimental career, but what should we do without them? How soon they convince us that it is not expedient to plant flowers, however luxuriant, with nothing on but their stalks, to insert bulbs with their roots upward, or twigs with their shoots downward. A single experiment convinced dear little

bright-eyed Willie that his ambitious enterprise
was a failure.

> " Dear little bright-eyed Willie,
>   Always so full of glee,
> Always so very mischievous—
>   The pride of our house is he.
>
> One bright summer day we found him
>   Close by the garden wall,
> Standing so grave and dignified,
>   Beside a sunflower tall.
>
> His tiny feet he had covered
>   With the moist and cooling sand ;
> The stalk of the great tall sunflower,
>   He grasped in his chubby hand.
>
> When he saw us standing near him,
>   Gazing so wonderingly
> At his baby-face, he greeted us
>   With a merry shout of glee.
>
> And when we asked what so pleased him,
>   He replied with cheeks aglow,
> ' Mama, I'm going to be a man,
>   And I've set myself to grow.' "

Pretty little gardens have been made for
pretty little folk, from dwarf evergreens and
diminutive flowers, sometimes including a tiny
rockery, and a lake almost large enough to

wash your hands in; but the children seem to prefer freedom to formality, and disorder to decorum. In one instance they made a rearrangement of the stones round the pond, to the great discomfort of "the Alpines," and in another they produced a representation of the ornamental waters in St. James's Park, by transferring the birds from their Noah's Ark to the pool. The exhibition, in which many of the feathered tribe were floating on their sides, and some with their legs in the air, must have been a painful spectacle to the patriarch and his family, who were contemplating the scene from the banks. It is better for all concerned, especially for the inmates of the ark, to give the children a remote corner in the kitchen garden where, with their barrow, and tools, and a nursemaid to restrain their deviations in search of unripe fruit, they may be monarchs of all they survey. There we will leave them for a very different scene.

R

CHAPTER XIV

The Town Garden [1]

"The weary woman stays her task
The perfume to inhale,
The pale-faced children pause
to ask
What breath is on the gale.

And none that breathe that sweetened air
But have a gentler thought,
A gleam of something good and fair
Across the spirit brought."

IN the telling of my own pursuits, it would be wrong to mislead the amateur gardener who may aspire to cultivate a beauty of flowers in a town garden, so I will therefore admit that I began my horticultural career as a professional. I was paid for my services. The arrangement

---

[1] For this pleasant addition to my book, I am indebted to a dear kinsman, who had the best Town Garden, surrounded by buildings, which I have ever seen.

made by my parent during the summer holidays was, I now believe, a one-sided affair. Sixpence a week was barely a living wage, but we had no union in those days to appeal to, and for this unequal remuneration I undertook to help mow (that is, pull the leading-string), weed, and water when necessary a "design of geraniums," and so, and this mainly (though not scheduled under the terms of agreement), to keep myself out of mischief.

Under these conditions I learned three things— a love of flowers, a knowledge of weeds, and a scorn for the geranium "bedded out." In this early love I have a memory of a star-raised bed of gentians, that rose out of the green grass, and hit you with its glorious blue blaze, while just over the "walk" there stood sentry a similarly shaped bed of "Gloire-de-Dijon" pegged down. A handsome couple, as I remember them, looking so well-bred, so undisturbed, in contrast to the other "things" a little further on, that were brought up on "cuttings," and looked it.

From home to another home of flowers, I had all the opportunity to let the love live on, and when I left the country manor that I loved so

well, to learn the town manners that I knew not
of, I was so well enthused that I determined to
face the old cant of "can't"—that you "can't
grow flowers in a town"—and you will let me
tell you, in my own simple fashion, how I sought
success. I remember that grand old gardener,
Mr. Ingram, under whose care the gardens of
Belvoir became a floral feast that should have
satiated the greediest enthusiast,—I remember a
remark he made to me, when I "thought" you
couldn't induce flowers to grow under trees:
"There are no such words as 'couldn't' and
'can't' in horticulture," and I went off with
him to see proof. In that lovely spring garden,
with its abundance of tall slender oaks, and its
bounty of wild cherry-trees, blossoming showers
of snow, you find the ground carpeted with
flowers to the tree trunk; and I need only mention *Omphalodes verna*, which looks like little
patches of the Mediterranean's bluest waters set
down there to rest awhile, with the double
white anemone peeping about in and out of the
blue, and many other charms that "can" if
you "will."

May I here mention one other main point

of gardening I learned from Mr. Ingram — I
practised it in my town garden even to greater
effect than I can now in my country borders—
the grouping of your colours. Put your blues,
your purples, your violets in a mass—your reds,
oranges, your pinks together, and so hit the eye
as it takes its first glance down your border, and
avoid magenta of any shade.

I must apologise for too many false starts;
the flag is down, and I am going straight for my
town garden. Let us dispose of the "front"—
I am opposed to playing with the front. My
own was a small one, with some old acacia trees,
chestnuts, a group of ferns, and a lawn, and I
would wish to have it so consisted. Where you
have greater extent, you will have more lawn—
for I pray you not to chop up your grass, so
restful to a town liver—and there insert little
beds of "bedding-outs." You will probably
have some old trees, fine fellows that grew their
growth when your town garden was practically in
the country, and upon them you rely to block
out the unseemly gable of your neighbour, or
it may be your own unsightly outbuildings or
high wall; but if there are gaps where the red

brick of this same wall grins through (and this is generally the case), then grow an ivy up it to cover its nakedness in the winter; and in the summer rely upon a broad patch of herbaceous things, with such plants as knot-weed (*Polygonum*), *Bocconia cordata*, some of the *Spiræa* tribe, to form your background, with your *Oriental poppies, Delphiniums, Phloxes, Pyrethrums*, and the like, as space may need, to brighten up the front rank. I have seen such belts of herbaceous groups, properly studied in colour and cared for with stakes, to stand out all through the summer as bright studs of colour in what has been beforetime a dreary land—for a town garden is so often and too often only that—because "you can't, you know, get things to do in a town," and you should add that you have never tried; for true as it surely is of so many plants, yet how great a libel upon so many others. I must enter a strong protest against the "evergreen" as unsuitable in a town to carry out the above responsible duty. I have never seen an "evergreen" in a town except he be of very mature age, planted in the days I have already alluded to, or as an established resident

of the cemetery, that has not scared me. All
legs and arms, with a trunk that is wasted for
want of warmth and fresh air, he only looks pre-
sentable when a creeper of violent growth has
spread up, around, and all over him; and the
way they shed their leaves all the year round is
indescribably indecent. I shall say no more.

We will now retire, if you please, to the back
regions—the kitchen garden. The first advance
I made upon this sanctuary of culinary failures,
is as fresh to my mind as though I had gone
back the nearly twenty years, when I stood there
meditating and musing on possibilities—and the
probabilities of some domestic discussion, if I
should ever grab it all, for my precious (once,
in later years, called "beastly") flowers. Thir-
teen years of patient labour outside (and of
loving patience inside) ere this was an accomplished fact, and one of the greatest generals
England ever had, has taken no shorter time
to plant the British flag once more on the walls
of Khartoum; and though I may garden under
conditions all so different, and attain a result
so much more picturesque, yet I shall never
again display that same glorious blaze of beauti-

ful colour, defying soot and smoke alike, and all other kinds of townly pests, proudly asserting, that "I can be a joy to you, in your town home, if you will only treat me fairly and squarely," and have patience.

I have told, I admit, the result of an extravagance, better described, perhaps, by a lady, an enthusiastic gardener, who came to see my show. "Why, the lad's mad"—that was all; but you need run no such risks; and I have since admitted (to avoid further abuse) that it *was* wicked of me to do these things; but then, after all, the town potato is as soap that has been left in a bath in error; the urban onion always has an ailment, just as you are going to store him; the carrot runs to "toes"; lettuce you have to conceal from that marauding rascal, the town sparrow; and the civic cabbage—oh, well! I'll tell you all about the cabbage. Only the other day I was judging at a flower show, and I had selected two very fine cabbages to stand first, when my professional coadjutor looked at them and at me, cut one of them open with a large clasp-knife, and, in a manner I thought unkind, he remarked, "The hinsides of a cabbage, sir,

is a very disappointing thing." So I think now—
and I probably had some such lurking idea of
the character of a cabbage, when, years ago, I
ordered him off my town premises.

Well, now, how to begin—to make the humble
start, on either side of the centre path of your
kitchen garden. I suppose you can spare me
six feet on either side. Dig this border well
over—really clean it—in the early autumn, and
put something into it—none of your light
"literary" trash, but good solid stuff. Why!
I remember a great and worthy man, looking at
my gardener laying on, as top-dressing for the
winter, some real "two-year-old," asking "if he
might have a bit done up in brown paper, just
to *show* his man." While you are digging,
go a-begging. Ask your country friend for a
bit of this or a bit of that; and if he or she
(the latter for choice) be a true gardener, he or
she will enjoy helping you in your start, and
the bits you pick up this way, seem to have so
much more grow in them, than the tiny bits
you get from the nurseries, and the price is
lower. I do not mean you are not to patronise
the nursery—you must, you will—but I advise

doing this later on, after you have made a start.
I am glad to say I give away barrow-loads in
the autumn, and am happier in mind and border
for the process; for division is good for the
plant, as it is for the beggar who gets it.

Now when you begin to plant your border,
do not of necessity put all your tall growing
things at the back, on the old principle,—nature
does not so plant. "Peeps" through a border are
prettier than a graduated scale; and if you have
my greed, you will want to widen the border
from time to time. You must please remember
where and what you plant, for when you dig in
your top-dressing in the spring, which has served
as your winter covering (and this should be done
with a short three-pronged fork), then you want
to know who is who and where he is—or the
damage may be serious.

Now the idea in a herbaceous border is to
keep up a succession of flowers from May to
October, and this can be done, though it takes
a few years to establish your plants, and have
them so closely grown together that no vacant
spaces occur; this is, of course, a strain upon
the productiveness of the soil, and you *must*

therefore be liberal with your winter management, and equally generous with your liquid manure throughout the summer—an invaluable supporter. To keep this crowd of plants in order, you should cut down each one immediately it has flowered, and freely "liquidate" the ground. The *Oriental poppy* and *Delphiniums* always give me a second bloom, but by the process I suggest, you help on the plants whose turn it is next to bloom; and let me here add, no border can be justly treated, unless you *stick* and *tie out* your plants, for if they are worth the trouble of growing, they are worth all the trouble of making the most of; and here again you give the next in succession the chance it needs.

I think I can tell pretty closely, how I managed my succession, and I shall of course confine myself to those flowers that I found to flourish, not merely grow, in a town.

Early spring flowers in a town garden are a delusion, for the necessary process of "stringing" crocuses, &c., to protect yourself against the common sparrow, is simply hateful; and I contented myself with the narcissus alone, which came peeping among the young layers of my old clove, of which I had broad bands up either side of the path; and after this herald of the spring, there should be no wait between the acts. "The Guards is out," was my old gardener's first declaration of advance, and I knew that the grand *Oriental poppy*, deep crimson with dark purple eye, had doffed his cap, and was in full dress uniform. He is a perfect pioneer, and I always managed to put him in company with the white lupine, and very well they marched together. The *Doronicum* is bright in its new gold, and the flags are all unfurling; and what a happy family they are! quite at home in the town, perhaps the best that I could grow in that border being *Iris ocroleuca* with its graceful spikes of white flowers, yellow-tongued, with that all useful, for ever flowering, double white *Rocket*, sweet as a stock; and now the *Spanish Iris* and the *Iceland poppies*, which I always mated in patches at conspicuous corners—and pretty rainbows of colour you get; and you may blend in with them, the dwarf *Campanulas*—white, blue, and the delicate lavender shade—for these little fellows, with the poppies, you may keep flowering all the summer through; but you need to water in the early morning, if the weather is hot. I have also tried *Ixias* to take the place of the *Iris*, but only occasionally with success in the town; I succeed well enough in the country. And after this there comes the reign of that princely tribe, the *Delphiniums*, a never-ending study in blues, with their centres of brown bees, black bees, black and white, black and tan, each one so distinct from his brother, but such a handsome stately family withal; and who other than the white *Foxglove* should be the attendant of this regiment of Blues!—and I may add this, that no herbaceous border can be complete without a goodly show of the white Foxglove, whose graceful nodding heads flash light through all your other colours; and therefore I would bid you welcome this wild friend from the woods.

Your border should now be at its best. The *Spiræas*, helping to lighten things up, with their graceful fronds and beards; the *Geums*, with their pretty red waistcoats and gold backs; the *Campanulas*—what a tribe!—from tiny *Muralis* to stately *Pyramidalis*; *Veronicas*, the scarlet

Lychnis (not too fond of town life), *Sidalceas,
Gaillardias, Inulas, Pyrethrums,* and the *Lilium
Croceum* always justified a place in my town
border, and this was practically the best I could
do in July; and I think I have your admission
that there is not much difficulty about it; and the
result was a joy to me, a pleasure and a surprise,
I believe, to many others. I tell again of Mr.
Ingram. He came to see this border at its best,
a solid square of flowers nearly three quarters of
an acre in extent, and he told me afterwards,
that he was "taken back" at such a display of
flowers in a town, but at the moment he said
nothing. My old gardener, Jacob by name,
stood silently awaiting the great man's verdict,
but as he said nothing, my faithful old man
(and no man ever loved a flower more faithfully,
for the flower's sake!) losing his patience, blurted
out, "Well! and what have you to say agin it?"
Mr. Ingram never forgot the look of anxiety on
old Jacob's face, and his reply was an invitation
to go in the following spring to see the Belvoir
gardens. I seldom missed going. I took my
"head" gardener with me, and when we had
shown him all, I asked him what he thought

of it, and he only said, "They keeps over twenty gardeners, and they keeps weeds too." The head gardener of Belvoir heard the remark and he groaned in pleasure, and Jacob was revenged.

I have been digressing. I have cut down the *Delphiniums*; I have "topped" the foxgloves; I have used the liquid pan; I have let in the *Hyacinthus candicans*, which have been carefully "sticked" to keep them straight; I have tied out some fine spikes of *Acanthus*, the *Penstemons* have had a care, the *Phloxes* too; I have cleared a way for *Anemone Japonica alba*, the *Eryngium Amethystinum*, in its coat of steel, with the *Echinops ruthenicus*, bobbing its blue heads; and I am ready for my autumn march. If your *Phloxes* are well chosen, in their lovely corals, their pinks and their rose shades, if you have a good clump of *Tritomas*, well stationed here and there, with the deep rose-coloured *Bergamot*, lightly relieved by the *Anemone*, and your old cloves are behaving themselves in the front rank, then the band may play, and your friends step in.

I have wondered since if the monthly rose, which I use largely here, with *Lobelia Victoria* to give me more red, would have done any good in the town. No well-ordained border should be without it.

In telling my story, I have omitted to mention many things I grew in my town border. I give you the main army. None of the Daisy tribe appreciate town life—the flowers are always imperfect in form, petals twisted, or some error of shape; even the *Anthemis*, an invaluable helper here, comes out imperfectly.

I think the only principle for town gardening is just this; find out what will grow, and multiply by three; what won't grow, don't try and divide, but add it to your list of failures, and *how* I have failed as you, in turn, I hope will fail; for if you don't, then it will be clear you are not trying to succeed. I think of some of these things. *Montbretia*, so easily grown here and so useful, if divided every two years, is only a rusty grass in the town; and how I struggled with the sweetly delicate, flesh-coloured *Ænothera marginata*, but what was the use?—and I could add a list of woe!

Time will teach you all these things, and it will tell you the secrets of a herbaceous border

—not only the succession of flowers, but the proper blending of colours as these successions come; and as you should be continually working among your plants — staying overgrowths, dividing where division is good—you will soon remember and remedy, where colours have clashed.

What more can I tell? My town garden was the joy of my heart and the rest of my brain for fifteen years, and I loved nothing better, specially on a Sunday evening "after church," than to walk around and amongst my flowers, with a working-man and his wife, and to tell them just what I knew; and their visits were frequent, for they always knew they were welcome. I have urged many just to have their few "hundreds" of garden ground edged with a border of flowers.

To all folks else, who would succeed with herbaceous plants in a town garden, my main advice is, "manure"; add patience, and the game is yours.

S. J. K. MARSLAND.

CHAPTER XV

Other Gardens

*" The whole range of nature is open to the gardener,
from the parterre to the forest, and whatsoever is agreeable
to the senses or to the imagination he may appropriate
to the spot he is to improve ; it is a part of his
business to collect into one place the delights which are
generally dispersed through different species of country."*
—WHATELEY.

*" Take thy plastic spade,
It is thy pencil : take thy seed, thy plants,
They are thy colours."*—MASON.

THERE are other gardens, to which for want
of space I can only refer briefly. There is the
SPRING GARDEN, with its

"Daffodil,
That comes before the swallow dares, and takes
The winds of March with beauty, violets dim.
But sweeter than the lids of Juno's eyes,
Or Cytherea's breath, pale primroses,
Bold oxlips, and the Crown Imperial
Lilies of all kinds, the flower-de-luce being one,"

with a long procession of lovely companions, crocus, hyacinths, tulips, scillas, iris, bulbous and tuberous plants of all denominations. Some gardeners devote a space to their vernal favourites exclusively, and when their place is empty, fill it with annuals or half-hardy plants; but where there is a Rock Garden, Wild Garden, and Herbaceous Border, we shall require no such reservation. The annuals will occupy those parts of the Herbaceous Border in which the bulbs have bloomed.

When there is a depth of dark, rich, fibrous, peaty mould, an AMERICAN GARDEN demands all our power of admiration for its infinite variety of splendid colours, in the massive bushes of the Himalayan Rhododendrons, in the brilliant hues of the Azaleas, and in the soft roseate tints of the Kalmia. They should be made a speciality wherever they prosper, but when they languish it is better to give them away before they take themselves off.

The ITALIAN GARDEN is so called because it is laid out in the geometrical style, which has always prevailed in Italy, from the time of Pliny in the first, to that of Lorenzo de Medici in the sixteenth century and onward. Horace Walpole denounces "the conceits of an Italian Garden,"—the same straight lines and angles, which might be intended to illustrate the propositions of Euclid, the same dead levels, tubs, and balustrades. Spenser describes in his "Færie Queene" a combination in which

> " All that Nature did omit,
> Art, playing Nature's second part, supplied."

but it is difficult to see in those Italian gardens where nature comes in. It can hardly be called a duet in which Art plays the organ, and Nature accompanies on the penny trumpet; when the servant assumes the mastery; when rigid rules and monotonous repetition are preferred to freedom and variety; when the straight canal is substituted for the meandering stream. "These mischiefs are occasioned not by the use but by the perversion of Art; it excludes instead of improving upon Nature, and therefore destroys the very end it was called in to promote." [1]

Italy has been called " the Garden of the World," in spite of its gardens. The Italian is not, never was, a gardener. If you see Art waiting upon Nature, that is, if you find a real garden, the owner is generally an Englishman or the gardener is a Scotchman. The most beautiful garden in Italy belongs to Mr. Hanbury at Mortola, even as in France, hard by, the best amateur rose-garden is that of Lord Brougham at Cannes.

I asked an old gardener whether he could tell me anything about DUTCH GARDENS, and he made answer, "They be bits o' beds with edgings o' box, and gravel walks, and four sloping banks forming a square outside, and they be pratty toys for children, and *very snug for varmint.*" The Dutch copied the Italian and French method, and a description of a garden in the reign of Trajan would have been equally appropriate to a garden in the reign of

1 Whateley's " Observations on Gardening."

William III., with the exception that the ponds, canals, dikes, and sluices of the latter were much more stagnant, muddy, and odoriferous. "The balancing system," by which every tree and ornament on the right hand had its counterpart on the left, was strictly adhered to; the same fantastic forms were reproduced in the evergreen trees.

It is a fact, nevertheless, that there is no country in which there is more enthusiasm or more practical knowledge about flowers. I can remember a time when there was a very large importation of rare trees and plants from the nurseries of Holland, and we all know that we are indebted almost exclusively for our lovely display of bulbous flowers in Spring to the growers at Haarlem and its vicinity. Horticultural Societies prosper on an extensive scale, and their exhibitions, at Ghent and elsewhere, are magnificent.

Best of all, this appreciation and enjoyment of beauty is universal. In the smallest house—and some of them, where land is dear, are so small that the main edifice is very little wider than the front door—the poorest artisan will

have his bit of garden, and he not only culti-
vates in their perfection the flowers which are
familiar to us, and those which, as a rule, de-
cline familiarity, but he produces those glorious
bulbs from the Cape which so rarely develop
their complete perfection in our borders, and
yet more rarely maintain it.

I have referred, in my book about roses, to
a GARDEN OF SWEET ODOURS, which had been
planted in the grounds of a country squire,
afflicted with blindness, so that, always fond of
his flowers, and still able to distinguish most
of those which were scentless by his touch, he
might have almost throughout the year their
sweet consolations. Theirs is an incense which
provokes no controversy, but commends itself
alike to the Puritan and the Roman nose—
sometimes with a powerful influence upon the
mind as well as upon the sense. Does not
the scent of the primrose, the violet, and the
cowslip sometimes transport us to the banks
and meads where first we found them, and restore, though but for a few seconds, the tender
grace of a day that is dead? Why do we sigh
when we have inhaled the breath of the first

hyacinth, the wall-flower, or of rose "La France"? Is it from mere anatomical causes, or from higher instincts? Do they recall the tender grace of a day that is dead? Do they mind us of departed joys, departed never to return?

Who shall define the source and the range of these associations. The cockney barber thinks that he pays a compliment to the blossom of the bean, when he compares its fragrance with the most delicious 'air oil; the schoolboy loves the scent of the heliotrope because it suggests cherry pie; while from the more imaginative and sentimental the sniff of a gardenia will evoke half a page of poetry. They are happiest to whom

"Sweet scents
Are the swift vehicles of still sweeter thoughts,"

to whom they bring the sweetest thoughts of all, of the frankincense and the myrrh, and the house that was filled with the odour of the ointment, and the sweet spices, and the golden vials of the saints.

It is, moreover, most helpful, most hopeful to such meditation, that the dismal desecration of our

burial grounds is no longer universal, and that
in the CEMETERY GARDENS, everywhere increasing, we can now find beauty, reverence, and peace ;
the ghastly hearse with its black feathers, like
ravens hovering over the dead, the huge hat-
band, *ludibrium ventis*, the hideous scarf, are
gradually disappearing, and with them the coarse
long grass, the rank weeds, the broken stones
of crowded graves, the massive square blocks of
stone with the iron palisades around, as though
there were some great distinction even after
death between rich and poor, although Diogenes,
when they found him groping in the charnel-
house, declared that he could see no difference
between the bones of the master and his slave.
If this ponderous excrescence,

"Monstrum, horrendum, informe, ingens,"

cannot be removed, there may be a modification.
Forty years ago I planted a weeping elm between
two of these quadrilaterals, and now the glimpses
of stone, faintly descried through the pendent
boughs, have a somewhat pleasing effect. Elsewhere in the same churchyard the broken head-
stones have been removed, and those which were

intact, but illegible or unsightly, have with the assent of their relations been laid even on the ground, which has been levelled and planted with evergreen and weeping trees, the silver-leaf or *Acer Negundo* and the vivid green of the *Acacia* contrasting with the *Irish Yew*. Snowdrops, Crocus, and Narcissus proclaim the resurrection of the spring, and rose *Felicité perpetué*, on the wall of the chancel, represents to the Christian his sure and certain hope. The desolate land has become a garden, in which every leaf and every flower, which fades in autumn, and reappears in spring, is a

"Sure pledge and proof that this is not the end."

It seems to be almost an instinct to associate a garden with Eden and Gethsemane, and living flowers with our dead :

"Lay her i' th' earth,
And from her fair and unpolluted flesh
May violets spring;"

and there are few sights more pathetic than that of the little children of the poor bringing posies of field flowers to their mother's grave. The ancient custom of "dressing the graves" on

Flower Sunday is still observed in Wales, Monmouthshire, and many other places. I went to preach some years ago at Farnsworth in Lancashire, and sleeping at the Vicarage on the Saturday night, was surprised to hear, soon after the dawn of day, " the clang of the wooden shoes," and the sound of many voices. Looking out I saw a crowd of both sexes, and almost all ages, placing flowers upon the graves of those whom they had loved long since and lost awhile. I saw husband and wife, themselves little more than boy and girl, stooping over the tiny grave of their firstborn, and the widow bringing her fatherless children, vainly endeavouring to repress that innocent mirth which so soon forgets its sorrow ; and I thought of Archbishop Trench's beautiful lines,

> " The glory which the earth puts on,
>   The child's unchecked delight,
> Both witness to a triumph won
>   (If we but read aright) ;
> A triumph won o'er sin and death,—
>   From these the Saviour saves ;
> And, like a happy infant, Faith
>   Can play among the graves."

And why should not Faith be strengthened, and

sorrow soothed, by these bright emblems of eternal life? Why should not God's acre be a garden, not only to humble us with shame with the thoughts of Paradise lost, but to exalt us with the hope of Paradise regained? Why should we not have Cemetery Gardens like those near Philadelphia, Boston, and Brooklyn, in the United States, parklike spaces tastefully laid out, pleasant homes and "fair havens," when the journey, and the voyage, is past? Sir Joseph Paxton has left an admirable example in the Cemetery Garden which he designed for Coventry, the city which he represented for many years in Parliament.

At some of our funerals in the present day there seems to be an excessive accumulation of costly crosses and wreaths; but it would be unkind to suppress these offerings of respect and affection; and that which seems to some a waste, may be given in the same spirit of generous love, which has an eternal record, and of which it was said, "She did it for My Burial." With no distrust as to sincerity of motives, the public notice, "No flowers," sounds always sadly in my ears.

Some arrange in a quiet nook their MEMORIAL GARDEN, in which they are happily reminded of their friends, who have planted or sent to them shrubs or flowers; and also of the places, some of them far away, from which they have brought the same souvenirs, the sweetest and prettiest of all. Such associations of our friendships and admirations, of those whom we have loved the best and of the scenes which have charmed us the most, with a life and beauty which endures for ever, keeps the memory of our attachments ever green, and our faith in the future always strong. There is a touching and a teaching pathos in a record by Alphonse Karr: "I had in a solitary corner of my garden three hyacinths, which my father had planted. He died before they came into bloom; but now every year the period of their flowering is to me a solemnity, a funereal and religious festival."

Even where there is no sign of life there is the remembrance and the hope; there is the sacred thought suggested by Mrs. Ewing, "I write *Resurgam* on labels, and put them wherever bulbs lie buried or such herbaceous treasures as die down, and are in consequence too often treated as mere mortal remains of the departed by the indiscriminating hand of some careless gardener."

All who have seen the SUB-TROPICAL GARDEN in Battersea Park must have admired the stately grace, the varied outline, the gigantic foliage, of the *Musa Ensete*, the *Ferdinandas*, the *Palms*, and the *Cannas:* but the space required for their growth and storage, the time and expense, make them possible only to Messrs. Crœsus and Co.; and though gardeners with a moderate extent of glass might furnish an annual supply for a bed, the result would not repay the outlay. Their room is better than their company, and there are hundreds of plants, quite as beautiful, which are perfectly able to take care of themselves without codling, or calling up young gardeners in a bitter frost from their warm bothies to mend their bedroom fires. After all, what poor specimens these emigrants are compared with their ancestors resident in their native land.

Addison makes a strong appeal in the *Spectator* for a WINTER GARDEN, and expresses his surprise that men who delight, as he does, in horticulture, do not follow his example in appropriating a large space to those trees which do not lose their leaves, such as the laurel, the hornbeam, and the holly. He affirms that these shrubs, when grown thick together, pro-duce an effect unspeakably cheerful; that you cannot imagine a more lively scene, and that they inspire the heart of the beholder with a sense of vernal delight; and though we may never have experienced this joy beyond word or thought, or felt at Christmastide this sweet exhilaration of the Spring, we all admire, in our more humble way, this verdure which never fails. It charms by contrast, like a smile on a sorrowful face, and should therefore be freely interspersed in our shrubberies, and in the large beds which I have suggested for our Ideal Garden.

I much prefer them thus distributed than grouped in a monotonous mass, and am no advocate for playing at Summer in a Winter Garden, gratefully content with the alternation of the seasons, and convinced that, with flowers as with friendships, a little absence makes the heart grow fonder. He who feasts every day feasts no day, and he who is addicted to sipping and " nipping " has an insatiable thirst. There are certain persons who seem to be always craving for that which is out of season. The flowers may be pale and scentless, the fruit and vegetables small and flavourless, but their precocity is supposed to disarm the critic, and to demand his admiration, which it does not always find. A proprietor who had many glass-houses, used almost exclusively for the "forcing" of flowers, fruit, and vegetables, and who claimed precedence over all in their premature production, was dining with a large party at the house of a friend. When the new potatoes, were handed round, and his neighbour remarked that they were the first he had seen, he exclaimed, in a tone which was heard by all, "I've had them for weeks." Whereupon his host remarked, "My dear friend, do not suppose for a moment that I should invite you to partake of any kind of food that was antiquated, common, or cheap,—those are *next year's new potatoes.*"

Let us be content, and more than content, with our evergreens, and alpines, and bright berries, until "the green leaves come again," and let us not forget that there is a Winter

Garden of such wondrous beauty that no words can describe, no pencil can delineate, no brush can paint it. It charms the eye with its graceful outlines, its perfect purity, its glittering sheen. No plumes from the ostrich, no brilliants from the mine can vie with those feathery, snow-clad branches as they sparkle in the midday sun, with the sky above them blue as the turquoise.

> "So cloudless, clear, and purely beautiful
> That God alone was to be seen in heaven."

This scene suggests the last garden to which I would refer, the largest, loveliest, least costly of all, EVERYBODY'S GARDEN, the land we live in. We concentrate the most beautiful trees, shrubs, and plants, which we can obtain, around our homes; we arrange them to the best of our ability in their natural site and soil, and they are, to all who appreciate beauty, a pure, un-failing joy; but they are only goodly stones from the great Temple of the Universe, leaves from a Tree which stretches out its boughs to the sea and its branches to the river, dust from the gold of Ophir. We must go into the Garden, which the Creator made very good; we must climb to the lichens of the high moun-

T

tain; we must look down from the roseate
heath and yellow hawkweed of the moorland
hills, upon the forests and the rivers, upon the
meadows and the orchards, and the valleys that
stand so thick with corn that they seem to
laugh and sing; we must follow the rivulets
which flow through ferns and mosses to the
lake; we must know the banks whereon the
primrose, and the violets, and the cowslip grow;
the woods and the groves in which the ground
is covered with anemones and hyacinths, blue-
bells and daffodils; the hedgerows with their
timber trees, flowering thorns, wild roses, honeysuckles, and clematis, "The Traveller's Joy";
the commons, with their glowing gorse; and we
shall find there a glory and a grace which
Art, horticultural or pictorial, may represent in
miniature, with spade or brush, and with a
success which charms because it reminds us of
realities which in their entirety no human power
could repeat. I have quoted Horace Walpole's
words about Kent, that "he left the fence, and
found that all Nature was a garden"; and all
true gardeners make the same discovery. I have
known persons who called themselves musicians,

but who did not seem to be interested in music when they were not performers; others, who were under the impression that they were horsemen because they possessed horses, although, when they rode abroad, they ostensibly suffered much discomfort both of body and mind, and had no more claim to the title than the *nouveau riche* in Toole's Play, who, when asked whether he was a sportsman, replied with indignation, "Course I am—always wor—kept ferrets reglar"; and others, alas, who claimed to be gardeners but were never heard to admire vegetation outside of their garden-gate. Impostors all! The musician only cares for the music which he has been taught to play; the clumsy rider wobbles on his steed because so many "swells" belong to the equestrian order; the proprietor approves his flowers because they are his property, and the visitors exclaim, "How pretty!"

He is no more a complete gardener than he who can only fish with a float is a "compleat angler," who says (I have heard him say it) that he only cares for orchids, or that if you will leave him his alpines, or his herbaceous border, or his roses, or his lilies, you may take the rest.

You will find *Head*-Gardeners in abundance willing and able to superintend hot-water pipes and gravel walks by the mile, and to supply flowers by the acre; but the *Heart*-Gardener makes a garden wherever plants will grow, and finds something beautiful go where he may. I do not say that a gardener must excel in every branch of floriculture, but that he must love *all* the flowers. He has received a divine commandment to consider the lilies *of the field*, and there is no more happy obedience.

Years ago I asked a friend, who had been staying in the neighbourhood of Hursley, whether he had seen Keble? and he replied, "Oh yes, we passed him one day when we were driving out, gazing at a flower or something by the wayside hedge, and looking as pleased as though he had just found a five-pound note." I knew that it was something far more precious in the eyes of the author of the "Christian Year," of one who wrote :—

"Sweet nurslings of the vernal skies,
    Bathed in soft airs, and fed with dew,
What more than magic in you lies,
    To fill the heart's fond view?

The stars of heaven a course are taught
Too high above our human thought;
Ye may be found if ye are sought,
And as we gaze, we know."

This faculty of adoration is given to us all,
and it brings a blessing to all who cherish it.
It keeps the child's heart in the brave man's
breast,

" And he wanders away and away,
With Nature, the dear old nurse,
Who sings to him night and day
The rhymes of the universe;
And whenever the way seems long,
And his heart begins to fail,
She sings a yet more wonderful song,
Or tells a more wonderful tale."

CHAPTER XVI

The Pedagogue's Farewell to his Pupils

" If little labour, little are our gains :
Man's fortunes are according to his pains."
                                    —HERRICK.

KIND words, which have made my heart glad, from those who have been induced by my enthusiasm to find a greater delight in their gardens, inspire the hope that this little volume may have some similar success, and may find readers who will not be angry—*lenit albescens animos capillus* — if I place them *in statu pupillari*, and offer, before we separate, a few more elementary hints.[1]

I. It will not be difficult for the young gardener to ascertain, from an inspection of his

[1] See page 152.

own garden and of those around him, from con-
sultation with experts, amateur and professional,
the plants which grow most luxuriantly in the
climate and soil of his district, and to these he
should give precedence. Should there be among
them one of those which by common consent are
acknowledged to excel in beauty, such as the
rose, or the lily, the iris, or the carnation, it
might be grown as a *specialité*; and it is a most
precious privilege gradually to form a complete
collection; but this should only be done where
there is ample room, and never to the exclusion
of those flowers which should be found in every
garden.

II. When he has decided what to grow, and
where to grow it, the question will arise, from
whence shall he procure his plants? He has not
learned as yet the more honourable, independent,
and economical methods of raising them from
cuttings and seeds, and therefore must purchase.
Let him go to the nearest nursery of good repute
—the shorter the time in which plants are out of
the ground the better—and make his selection.
If to procure that which he requires it is necessary to go further afield, let him remember Sir

William Temple's admonition and "draw his trees from some nursery that is upon a leaner and lighter soil than his own, without which care they will not thrive; and life is too short and uncertain for their oft renewing." Let him not be tempted by the "tremendous sacrifices" of Cheap Jacks, but deal with merchants "of credit and renown," following the rule of Buckstone, the actor, who, when certain rabid sectarians desired to rent his theatre, informed his correspondents that "he confined himself to the legitimate drama." He must pay a just price for a good article, but it is, eventually, as superior in appearance and durability as double-milled cloth to shoddy.

III. October and November are the best months for planting, except for evergreens, which I was advised by an authority, *nulli secundus*, Mr. Robert Marnock, to remove in August, when the ground is warm to cherish the roots. These roots will be handled tenderly, carefully spread in ample space, firmly covered with congenial soil, and copiously watered, by those that love them. I saw a brainless lout, who described himself as a jobbing gardener, take out his knife and cut off large pieces from the roots of a plant, which was too large for the hole he had dug to receive it, before I had time to interfere. I could only inquire, "If you were buying garden gloves, and the first which you tried were too short for your hand, should you cut off the tips of your fingers, or should you ask for a longer pair?"

Each shrub or plant should have a stick or stake to support it, lest it become *ludibrium ventis*, with a "tally" affixed or adjoining. These tallies have vexed my spirit for more than half a century, and I have finally decided in favour of strong slips of metal, nine inches in length by one in breadth, with a figure or figures embossed on the top. These figures are noted in a book kept by the proprietor, with a duplicate for his gardener. They are always in their place, and legible.

IV. I must earnestly implore the young gardener not to be wise in his own conceits. Of all the prides since Lucifer's attaint, there is not one more disastrous to progress and success than that which will never acknowledge ignorance, and would rather remain in darkness than ask a neighbour for a light. I confess in sackcloth and ashes that I was misled for the greater portion of my life by this moral obliquity, and I am sure that, if I had resisted and overcome it in my youth, I should have quadrupled my store of useful knowledge. Nor can I derive much solace from the fact that this stupid arrogance is a common disease: so is the Influenza. It wastes time, loses opportunity, and gets in other people's way, like a loafer at the corner of the street.

When I was at Limerick with John Leech, we went forth from our hotel to see some object which had been commended for our inspection, under the directions of the waiter, which we forgot in five minutes. Trusting to the intuitions of our omniscience, we wandered on, disdaining to ask for information, until after an hour's aberrations we found ourselves in front of our hotel. It was, of course, impossible to acknowledge to the waiter, who regarded us, in deference to the famous artist, with reverent admiration, that we were not absolutely exempt from human error, and we actually undertook a second expedition under the same conditions, and, after a more brief period of absence, the same result. Then we came to the conclusion that the object of our search was not worth seeing, and took rest in our inn.

Let the young gardener be continually asking his seniors to tell him that which he does not know. If he asks in humility, and does not transgress the boundaries of good taste, as for instance by inquiring from victorious exhibitors the secrets of their success, he will find, as a rule, a sympathy ready to help. Mr. Ruskin writes, that "a child is always asking questions, and wanting to know more. Well, that is the first character of a good and wise man at his work. To know that he knows very little; to perceive that there are many above him wiser than he; and to be always asking questions, wanting to learn, not to teach." The young gardener should learn these words by heart; for there was never an age when the warning was more needed, or less heeded, *O formose puer, nimium ne crede colori*—"Beautiful young man, don't be bumptious!"

V. The neophyte should seek instruction not only from the lips but from the writings of the expert. First I commend to his perusal and possession

"THE ENGLISH FLOWER GARDEN,"
BY W. ROBINSON.

It is a work which could have only been achieved by a pure love of the beautiful, by a righteous disdain of deformities, by a devoted service,

"Upborne with indefatigable wings
Over the vast abrupt;"

and it is accepted as the most comprehensive and reliable book upon its subject. It expresses pleasantly, lucidly, and concisely, a most sincere and accomplished zeal, and with an abundance of exquisite illustrations the artist accompanies the author, as some skilful pianist a song.

I have referred to Miss Jekyll's fascinating volume on "Wood and Garden." It is unique in its alliance of the practical with the picturesque.

"The History of Gardening in England, by Alicia Amherst," is another *magnum opus*, a standard work of great research, full of interesting information about gardens and gardeners, from the times of the Romans to our own.

I have only space to mention, with the brief

commentary that they are all charming books,
" In a Gloucestershire Garden," by Canon Ellacombe, " Pot-Pourri from a Surrey Garden,"
by Mrs. C. W. Earle, " Days and Hours in a
Garden," " The Garden's Story, " A Year in
a Lancashire Garden," " Ros Rosarum ex hortu
Poetarum," and " Elizabeth in a German Garden."
There are, I believe, many more of much merit,
but I have not seen them.

Of books on Gardens, anterior to those I have
mentioned, I would select " Parkinson's Paradise," " Gerarde's Herbal," " Walpole's Essay on
Modern Gardening," " Whateley's Observations,"
" Redouté on the Rose," with a caution to the
buyer to ascertain prices before investment ; and
of later date, Loudon's " Encyclopædia of Gardening," " Paxton's Botanical Dictionary," and
" Kemp's How to Lay Out a Garden."

The young disciple should subscribe to a
weekly horticultural paper, and should study the
catalogues. A mutual interest in these catalogues has been the source of many friendships,
and of yet more intense attachments. An enthusiastic gardener told me that he went, when
a bachelor, to visit a college friend, who had two

lovely sisters. He saw them, in the distance, going into the house as he drove up the avenue, and when he entered the hall he found that one had placed a basket with garden-gloves, scissors, and a catalogue on the table, and the other had deposited a novel by an authoress of the earth, earthy. He was irresistibly drawn in the direction of the basket, but when he touched the catalogue, a huge dog growled at him from below, "and I am not sure," he added, "that he ever quite forgave my intrusion, though his owner became my wife."

VI. The gardener must wage war without armistice against weeds, slugs, aphis, dirt, and disorder.

VII. In time of drought he must water freely, soaking, not sprinkling, the soil.

VIII. He must be ever grateful, and in his gratitude generous to others. Let him not forget, amid his happy enjoyments, the hospital and the sick man's home. "Freely ye have received, freely give."

CPSIA information can be obtained at www.ICGtesting.com
Printed in the USA
LVOW041519080512

280867LV00005B/58/P